PATTERNS,
NOT PADLOCKS

D0168833

By the same author:

Heaven in Ordinary
Prayer in the Shadows

PATTERNS,
NOT PADLOCKS

For parents
and all busy people

Angela Ashwin

Guildford, Surrey

Copyright © Angela Ashwin 1992

British Library Cataloguing-in-Publication Data. A catalogue record for this book is available from the British Library.

Published by Eagle, an imprint of Inter Publishing Service (IPS) Ltd, 59 Woodbridge Road, Guildford, Surrey GU1 4RF.

All rights reserved. No part of this publication may be reproduced or transmitted in any form or by any means, electronic or mechanical, including photocopying, recording or any information storage and retrieval system, without either prior permission in writing from the publisher or a licence permitting restricted copying.

In the United Kingdom such licences are issued by the Copyright Licencing Agency, 33–35 Alfred Place, London WC1E 7DP.

Typeset by The Electronic Book Factory Ltd, Fife, Scotland. Printed in the UK by HarperCollins Manufacturing, Glasgow.

Cover illustration by Paul Judson.

ISBN 0 86347 088 2.

For Emily

Acknowledgements

Many people have helped me during the writing of this book. In particular I would like to thank Hannah and Ben Gibbons for allowing me to take photographs of them, and for letting their mother, Kay, read through the manuscript and give me her perceptive comments.

I am immensely grateful to my husband and children for their unflagging support during the writing of this book. I would also like to thank Joyce Huggett for her wisdom and kindness, and David Wavre of *Eagle*, whose encouragement and practical assistance have made all the difference.

Biblical quotations are from the Revised Standard Version unless otherwise stated:
(GNB) The Good News Bible.
(JB) The Jerusalem Bible
(NEB) The New English Bible
(NIV) The New International Version
(NRSV) The new Revised Standard Version
All cartoons are by Paul Judson ©

Contents

Foreword

I first met Angela Ashwin through her book, *Heaven In Ordinary.* This book impressed and attracted me because it seemed so obvious that, although the author was a busy vicar's wife and the mother of small children, she was also consumed with an unquenchable thirst for God. This thirst prompts her to find ways, to use her own words, of finding Christ in the middle of chaos.

So when the young mums in the church where I used to worship began asking questions like: 'Is it possible to be a person of prayer and the mother of toddlers?' I thought of Angela. Would she be willing to show how young parents and other equally busy people can establish a meaningful prayer life?

I telephoned her. Our minds met. Subsequently she visited my home to discuss the contents of this book. When the manuscript was almost finished, she also came to meet 'my' young mums. I watched their reaction as she presented some of the material from her manuscript. Looks of relief and release gradually crept across first one face, then another, then another. From the questions they asked afterwards and the appreciative, affirming comments they made, it became apparent that the session had been an important eye-opener. As their perception of prayer changed, guilt evaporated and they were brought to the brink of a new discovery – that prayer is not a duty to be performed but an adventure we can enjoy no matter how busy we are.

Sensing their reaction, I waited eagerly for the completed manuscript. It arrived one morning while the removal men were carrying the furniture out of our home. My husband and I were in the middle of moving from our Rectory to Cyprus via a small cottage in Derbyshire. Surrounded by packing cases, I read the manuscript and thanked God for the timing of its arrival. 'It's a long time since I qualified for the title "young mum",' I thought, 'but the pressures of moving house seem to be similar to the pressures Angela describes. So, there and then, I put into practice some of the prayer suggestions she makes, applying her principles to my situation. She suggests, for example, that parents should not necessarily wait until the house is tidy before they settle down to pray. Rather, when a few quiet moments present themselves, they should be content to sit down in the middle of a room full of toys and pray there if necessary. So I sat down in the middle of a room full of packing cases and found that a few concentrated moments with God brought to me renewal and strength and a much-needed in-tuneness with God's presence.

And I loved the cartoons Angela specially commissioned to illustrate her book. They reminded me of the author's own delightful sense of humour and her determination, on the one hand to take God and his Gospel seriously but flatly to refuse to take herself too seriously.

That is not to say that her book is trite. Far from it. There are profound and deeply moving moments hidden in its pages – both through what she writes and to be discovered by those who take the trouble to experiment with some of the prayer suggestions she makes.

One of the young mums who heard Angela speak at the meeting I have described, told me that she was going home with a whole variety of new prayer avenues to explore, but she added the rider with which I am certain that Angela would agree, that she would also need continually to draw on the enabling and inspiration of the Holy Spirit if she was to benefit in any lasting way from the new insights. How true! It is my prayer that readers of this book, no matter how busy they are, will seek a regular, fresh anointing of God's Spirit and that he, in turn, will open their eyes and touch their hearts to discover for themselves the richness of the contents of these pages.

Joyce Huggett
July 1992

INTRODUCTION

In the 1950's, a certain church ran a mission which they planned to call 'Christ or Chaos'. Fortunately someone pointed out that such a title could easily be misunderstood, and drive people into either fear or despair: fear that 'chaos' would be their punishment if they didn't respond as they should, or despair of ever being good enough for Christ, because their lives *were* in a state of chaos. So an alternative title was found: 'Christ **in** Chaos.'[1] And *that* could easily have been the title of this book!

The chaotic, marvellous and exhausting experience of being new parents disrupts even life's most basic ingredients, such as meals and sleep, and certainly puts a spanner in the spiritual works for most of us who try to pray. Regular 'quiet-times' fly out of the window for fathers and mothers alike. God seems to be lost somewhere underneath the piles of chores, and our inclination to pray drops to zero with alarming frequency. Guilt – usually misguided – is the first enemy to attack our interior landscape; this is closely followed by discouragement, and the temptation to give up prayer altogether.

When in past years I have felt like this, I have been helped by a friend who:

a. understood

b. enabled me to interpret my experience in relation to my faith, and

c. suggested some practical ideas and initiatives, so

that my hectic life could reflect the things which I believed to be important.

In this book I hope to offer that kind of support to parents, and to explore some pathways into prayer which lead *through* the nappy-changes, teething-troubles and playgroups, rather than *round* them.[2]

Parents of small children are not, of course, the only people to experience constant pressures. You may have a tiring job, or a sick or elderly person to care for at home. Perhaps you are deeply involved in voluntary work, or are coping with a teenage family. All such situations can reduce your time and energy for prayer. I hope, therefore, that the thoughts and suggestions in this book will speak to any reader who wants to pray in the middle of a busy and demanding life.

When you do find an opportunity to be alone and quiet with God, it may help to have a theme or focus to lead you into stillness with him. So at the end of some chapters there are suggestions about how you could use portions of the text, and certain pictures, when a space for quiet prayer presents itself.

*I had to learn to sit down in the
middle of the rubble and debris.*

CHAPTER 1

Rescued From Guilt

See what love the Father has given us, that we should be called children of God; and so we are. (I John 3:1)

'Non-existent!' exploded my friend, as she knelt on the carpet surrounded by the remnants of the toddlers' tea and scattered heaps of toys. 'My prayer-life disappeared when this one was born,' she added, hugging her eldest child. 'And I feel so *guilty*!'

The arrival of babies affects the lives of parents so drastically that any fixed schedule of prayer will be extremely difficult to follow. Finding 'quiet times' is a forlorn hope when both 'quiet' and 'time' are at a premium. Suppose we make a resolution to pray before the rest of the family wakes up. It's as much as we can do to drag ourselves out of sleep for the baby's first feed, or for the toddler's early-morning burst of energy, without trying to get up even earlier. Then we either have a hard day out at work, or stay at home with never-ending chores, children to ferry to playgroup and school, babies and toddlers to watch, and meals, clinics, and shopping to fit in, not to mention all our other commitments. In the evening there may still be jobs to be done, and we are so exhausted at the end of it that we collapse into bed with the uneasy sense that yet another day has slipped by without any time given to God.

As this pressurised life continues, there is a danger that we could despair of *ever* being prayerful people again. At this point warning lights should flash, because we are tempted to stop trying, and to cut ourselves off altogether from a living relationship with God. We urgently need to be reassured that God understands our situation, that he still loves us, and that he will show us different patterns of praying which make sense in our new and busy circumstances.

If we are already spiritually undernourished, the last thing we must do is starve ourselves further. We need help because prayer has become just one more demand in an already over-loaded day, and guilt has begun to paralyse our initiative. We feel bad about letting God down, yet we cannot find the inner resources to do anything about it. Discouraged and weary, we have fallen into an apparently God-forsaken ditch, out of which we cannot climb alone. Fortunately rescue is at hand, with both the first aid and the emergency supplies that we need.

First aid
When our own children are miserable, we instinctively take them into our arms, whatever the reason for their unhappiness. We don't hold them at arm's length until we have established how much of their distress is their own fault. We love them and cuddle them first, because they matter to us, and *then* we help them to sort things out. In the same way, God holds us in his love when we feel wretched and unworthy, breathing his life and healing into

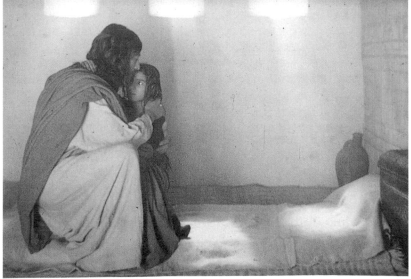

us at the deepest point of our unhappiness, and gently inviting us to let go of any crippling guilt that we have been dragging around. He is hardly going to be less loving with us than we are with our own children!

God has, after all, given us our family and the responsibilities that go with it. He knows and understands how we feel, and is with us in the middle of it all, inviting us to meet him here. It is as if he says to us, 'I know how your life has been changed by having children. Guilt-feelings over failed rules of prayer have nothing to do with me. I know that you are vulnerable at the moment, but I am holding you in my love, and I will never abandon you, however low you fall in your own esteem. Will you let me pour my love into you, now?'

One way to respond when we are in our ditch of discouragement is to whisper or think a name such as, 'Lord,' 'Love,' 'Loving Spirit,' or 'Abba Father,' and to rest in the knowledge that we are totally accepted, forgiven and loved. As a friend of mine with young children wrote recently in a letter, 'I now realise that I don't need a structured rule of prayer to make God love me, nor do I have to work to be special to him.'[1]

First-aiders keep the person they are helping warm, by wrapping them in a blanket. This is a useful image in our praying. The sense that God enfolds us in his love, like a garment, goes back to the medieval saint, Julian of Norwich;

'I saw that He is to us everything that is good and comfortable for us. He is our clothing which for love enwraps us, holds us, and all encloses us because of his tender love, so that He may never leave us.'[2]

Pondering these marvellous words may help to restore our hope when we feel inwardly cold and separated from God's love.

A Hot Drink of Light.

Imagine a hot and restoring drink pouring down the gullet of someone who is injured and shivering with cold. And then picture the warm liquid as light flowing into the dark places inside. Perhaps that person is you! Perhaps you, too, need a restoring draught of Christ's light. Not only is Jesus the light of the whole world (John 8:12), he is also the light of *your* world and of *your* life. In your imagination, allow the divine light to seep into every part of you; relax the back of your neck and throat, and feel the light warming, healing and envigorating your body, mind and spirit. On a demanding day, you could pinpoint certain moments when you will again pause to absorb Christ's light, e.g. when you brush your hair, take the first sip of tea, or turn on the tap to wash up. Even in the most crowded day, there are occasions when we do stop rushing round, and they can become important moments of refreshment if we use them like this.

Long-Term Rehabilitation.

Short-term first aid and nourishment are vital, but we still need to be carried right away from our chilly ditch of despair, or we may slip back into it. We need to be freed from the distorted idea that God is a stern, Victorian head-master who will make us grovel for not sticking to a fixed time of daily prayer. God is *with us* in our life as parents, and not 'out there', pointing an accusing finger from a distance. As the Psalmist reminds us, God loves us tenderly, 'as a father pities his own children,' (Ps. 103:13). So if we can now pick ourselves up and let go of inappropriate prayer-rules which paralyse us with guilt, we may become more free to explore new ways of staying close to God, even in the middle of domestic din and constant chaos.

Two important guidelines have stood me in good stead:

1. *Every moment is God's moment; we can pray at any time and in any place, no matter what we are doing.*
2. *Sometimes we need space in which simply to be alone with God; we don't know when this will be possible, so the timing of our periods of quiet will be more a surprise than an appointment.*

1. Praying at any time

Before you read any further, I invite you to pause and tell God what you feel you most need at this moment.

You have just experienced the fact that any moment can be prayerful, however ordinary the circumstances. Perhaps you have also exposed a dark or difficult part of yourself, which can now be opened up to God's light and warmth. Your need may have been as immediate as 'a good night's sleep', or as serious as 'inner peace'; it may have been as hopeful as 'deeper trust in God', or as despairing as 'something to laugh about'. Whatever it was, take it, hold it, and offer it as your gift to Christ, who always comes to us at the point of our need. Prayer starts where we are now, and not in some rigid text-book of pious observances that are always beyond our grasp.

It may be that the need you expressed was a *cri de coeur* about life's relentless demands, and the lack of time to relax or pray in peace. This is a particularly valuable offering to make to God, because it shows that you long for him even when you are preoccupied with all the work that has to be done. Wanting God is, after all, the heart of prayer. So, when you say, 'Lord, I wish I could pray,' you *are* praying, whether you are full of resentful frustration, or whether you are content but just incredibly busy.

Praying with unlikely ingredients

Sometimes we can learn to pray with the very experiences that we had seen as blockages to our spiritual life. You might find it helpful to ask yourself, 'Which bit of my daily activity seems the most remote from prayer and faith?' Try opening this up to Christ now.

The surprise is that the part of your life which you had regarded as counter-productive to prayer has become the place where Christ is nearest to you, because he always comes to us at our point of need. The apparently God-less area you identified is now a door on which Christ is knocking, and which he is waiting for you to open (Rev. 3:20). There is no padlock on this door; it opens easily from the inside as soon as you are prepared to expose your life to him.

In the Gospels, the people who were closest to Jesus tended to be those who were not cluttered up with their own 'spiritual achievements', and who were often considered to be disreputable by the religious leaders of the time. 'Why does he eat with tax collectors and sinners?' complained the Pharisees (Mark 2:16). Jesus does not wait until we are in a 'fit state' to receive him, nor is he biding his time until our life is less hectic. Our worst moments can become prayer as much as our best ones, and he will use our experience of sleepless nights, doctors' queues and household pandemonium to bring us closer to him, if we will let him.

Just as our love for our children remains constant, even when caring for them becomes demanding and difficult, God also loves us steadily, through thick and thin. What matters is that we turn to him *as we are now,* in our incompleteness and imperfection. The kind of praying explored in this book is not a temporary survival mechanism to see us through a sticky patch until we can start praying 'properly' again. Praying with a food-bespattered high-chair and a toddler with a temperature *is* proper praying.

2. Spaces for God alone

Spaces for concentrating on God alone are important, but opportunities for this are a rare treat when we have small children. Yet there is still a way of finding times of quiet, while, at the same time, avoiding perpetual guilt over broken prayer-rules.

If we were brought up to pray at the same time every day, we may have a sneaking feeling that this is the only real way to please God. But our lifestyle now makes that impossible. Perhaps we are placing too much security in our old scheme of praying, as if our relationship with God *depends* on it. Rules of prayer are only meant to be tools to help us grow closer to him. When circumstances change, the tools must change too. If the rules become ends in themselves, they turn into padlocks, imprisoning their victims either in pride (for law-keeping) or in despair (for law-breaking). This is why Jesus so often argued with the Pharisees about their obsession with the letter of the law, which smothered both compassion and common sense (e.g. Mark 2:23–28, 3:1–6). Jesus could see that the law had become a task-master rather than an enabler in Israel's spiritual life. And we need to be as free as he was, distinguishing between rules which reinforce the guilt syndrome, and good patterns which capture the essential heart of praying, which is reaching out to God.

What, then, are we to do, if our young family or heavy work-schedule prevents us from sitting down alone on a regular basis? Where do we start in the search for opportunities to 'be still and know' that God is God?

The unexpected gift

Instead of seeing quiet-times as *our* gift to God, we can turn the idea back to front. They are *God's gift to us*, which he gives when and as he wills. All we have to do, therefore, is wait and see when the spaces occur – and then respond!

This discovery came as an enormous relief to me during the first few weeks after the birth of our oldest child. Before she arrived, I had assumed that I would be able to continue with my tidy prayer-slot every morning. Some hope! I have never felt such a mixture of delight and alarm as when I had a new daughter; as well as rejoicing I was also panicking because my old ways of praying were slipping down the plughole of exhaustion and chaos.

It was wonderful to realise that I could let go of my former rule of prayer, and that to do this was *not* to abandon my loyalty to Christ. As the burden of guilt over this gradually lifted, I began to enjoy the sense of anticipation, waiting to see when a chance for solitude with God would turn up. It might be daily, or it could be less frequently. A new challenge had now presented itself: would I be obedient enough to take the chance for space with God when it came my way? Or would I convince myself that I really *must* finish the ironing, or write that letter, or do any other job that was important but not urgent? This was a real test of faithfulness, and became a struggle over priorities which continues to this day!

We obviously have to watch that we do not abuse our new-found freedom. Abandoning an inappropriate prayer-rule is quite different from finding excuses not to pray. If we never pause to focus our love and attention on God, our relationships and work are bound to suffer, as well as our state of heart and mind. Certainly we can pray while we are busy; much of this book is about doing just that. But sometimes God wants our undivided attention, and the onus is on us to take the opportunities when they arise. We need a realistic framework for our praying, a minimum commitment which we are likely to keep, rather than an over-optimistic rule which we will probably break. Then light can break through.

How much time?
It is easy to be too ambitious in the amount of time we promise to spend with God when a space appears. A friend said to me recently, 'I find I *cannot* pray

during those precious gaps when the baby's asleep, because it's my only chance to tidy up and get on with the housework!' It turned out that she was thinking in terms of half-an-hour, which was an unrealistic length of time in the present stage of her life. When I suggested ten minutes she was much relieved, and the prospect seemed quite different.

It helps to have a friend with whom we can talk about our situation, and try to work out which promises would only end up as guilt-inducing padlocks, and which would be right for us now. (We can always review things later, when circumstances have changed.) For many people, the best way to do this is to have a coffee and a chat regularly with a 'soul-friend' who also has a young brood, and to let the chaos carry on at your feet as you talk. Struggling to be a Christian can be a lonely business at the best of times, and mutual support between like-minded people is a key way in which God helps us. Other people prefer to talk to a 'spiritual director', who can be clergy or lay, monk or nun – anyone, in fact, who prays and can accompany others on their spiritual journey. Most of us need the reassurance of discussing our experience with someone who will hold our hand on the way.

If you are thinking that there is *never* a space in your life, I would suggest that you watch out for the next gap of a few moments that comes out of the blue, even if it's only two or three minutes' peace. It *will* appear, at some point! When it comes, keep very still, and hear God saying to you,

'I am the Lord; I am, beyond time;
I am with you now.
With me, a thousand years are like a single day,
and a few moments can be a taste of eternity.
Let go of busy thoughts,
and let me love you,
now,
as I love you
in and through all time.'

When we only have a very short period of quiet, it is amazing how it can expand in our consciousness and take on an importance out of all proportion to the number of minutes it contained. (Some practical ideas about how to use spaces with God are given at the end of this and several other chapters.)[3]

Another lesson I learned when the children were small was to sit down in the middle of the crumbs and the debris, and seize the chance to pray there and then. No quick tidying up! God doesn't require a hoovered carpet before we can open up to him, and we may lose the opportunity to enjoy his presence uninterrupted if we try to clear up first.

Sometimes our external behaviour mirrors things that are going on inside us. If you feel that you cannot pray when the place is a mess, it may be that you are reluctant or afraid to come to God until you're 'all cleared up and respectable' inside as well. In that case, literally sitting down to pray when all around you is in disarray might help you to accept that God does love you *as you are*, mess, muddle and all.

We have a unique opportunity
Christianity is a journey into freedom, not a straight-jacket of piety, and having small children sets the scene for us to discover this in a unique way. Since life is so unpredictable, we can become more open to the way God is reaching out to us at every moment, and realise that his life-giving energy lies behind our children's glorious outbursts of creativity – even when bright splodges of paint end up on the floor as well as on the drawing-paper. Through sheer necessity, we look for ways of keeping a thread of communion with God right through the day, and taste the freedom of sharing God's delight in giggles and silly games and the hilarious moments that our children give us. And these ways of praying might never have occurred to us if we hadn't had a family.

A final thought. Suppose you try the various suggestions in this book and still reckon that you are getting nowhere with prayer. The last thing you must do is to feel guilty. God accepts *all* our attempts to pray, however unsatisfactory we may think them. It is especially when we are helpless and despondent, and feel that God is a thousand miles away, that his love is unshakeable and all-embracing. 'As one whom his mother comforts, so I will comfort you,' says the Lord (Isaiah 66:13).

In her novel *Leaning on a Spider's Web*[4], Jennifer Rees Larcombe tells the story of a young woman, Emmie, who decides, with some trepidation, to go to church one Sunday morning. Emmie is in an emotional turmoil, and is looking for something which she feels is lacking in her life at present. On the way, she prays that God will somehow show her that he doesn't reject her, as her own father had done in the past. As she draws closer to the church, thinking that she must be mad to be doing this, Emmie passes the vicarage garden, where the vicar's two small daughters are playing in the sunshine, wearing next to nothing. Their grandmother is keeping an eye on them, because their mother was tragically killed some months earlier.

Emmie wavers at the steps of the church, but is swept inside by a kind and gentle friend. She finds the beginning of the service difficult, but then something happens. Emmie is watching the patterns made by the sunlight pouring through the stained-glass windows, while everyone else is deep in prayer. Suddenly she notices a little, tearful child at the church door, coming in silently on bare feet, and heading straight for her father, the vicar, at the front.

The little girl has obviously fallen down, because her knees are dirty and bleeding, and in the process of eluding her grandmother and rushing to find her father, she has lost her knickers.

For Emmie this is a vital moment. In this distraught child she sees herself, denied affection in the past by her own father, and now longing to be loved by God. She waits on tenterhooks to see what will happen, as the tiny, naked figure runs silently up the aisle in the middle of this respectable Anglican service.

As soon as the vicar sees his daughter, he smiles and instantly reaches out to pick her up and enfold her lovingly in the yards of white material of the church surplice he is wearing. The novel continues,

'Never before in the history of St. Mark's had a vicar led worship and preached a full-length sermon with a small child fast asleep in his arms . . . Emmie knew she would never be the same person again. Like that child, she had come into church feeling distressed – looking for comfort and protection. Through the way the vicar had responded to his daughter, God had given her the sign for which she had asked. She knew she was accepted and loved.'

*   *   *

Even when my old and familiar ways of praying are taken away from me,
I am never taken away from you, Lord.
You are here, reaching out to me,
loving me now.

Even when I am denied a space to be quiet with you,
there is still a space inside me, Lord,
an inner room where you are waiting for me,
and which I can enter at any moment.

Even when I feel miserable and worthless
I am still precious in your eyes,
because I am your child,

and you are waiting to open your arms and embrace me.

A SPACE FOR STILLNESS

Before you start, relax any muscles in your body which are tense and tight, especially in the back of your throat, neck and shoulders. Listen to the sounds around you, gently letting go of the noise and chatter in your head. Then turn to one of the suggestions below, open and ready to receive whatever God may give to you.

Ψ Ponder slowly the words of Julian of Norwich on page 18, 'I saw that he is to us . . .' Feel the love of God enfolding your whole being, and let his warmth and gentleness flow into you.

Ψ Look at the pictures of Jesus healing Jairus's daughter (page 17). Read the section headed *First Aid* (pages 16–18) and listen to God's invitation, 'Will you let me pour my love into you, now?'

Ψ Read the section *A Hot Drink of Light* on page 19. Follow the suggestion for imaginative praying here.

Ψ Read pages 21 to 22 in Chapter 1, *Praying with Unlikely Ingredients*, and open up to God any negative or frustrated feelings you may have. Write down any area or areas in your life which make it hard to be prayerful. Cup the paper in your hands and offer it to Christ, as a way of putting your life into his hands. Look at the picture on page 25, and ask that God's light will break through the darkness in your life.

Ψ Read the story from the novel *Leaning on a Spider's Web*, on pages 28 to 29. Absorb the fact that God loves you in the same way as the little child is loved here.

Ψ Slowly say the prayer on pages 29 and 30. Remember that you are indeed cherished in God's eyes as a beloved daughter or son.

Ψ If you have only a short amount of time to yourself, use the prayer on page 26, 'I am the Lord . . .' Ask that this brief taste of stillness with God will strengthen you as you go back to the day's activity.

CHAPTER 2

Life's Relentlessness

Whatever you are doing, put your whole heart into it, as if you were doing it for the Lord. (Col. 3:23 NEB)

Some baby-care books used to make me wonder whether to laugh or cry. First they presented you with a daily timetable in which everything worked like clockwork. Feeds, cleaning, shopping and cooking fitted neatly into the morning, and an 'after-lunch rest' was guaranteed. After an equally well-ordered afternoon, it was assumed that you would have an early night before baby's 2 a.m. feed!

In my experience, life is just not like that. Although a tiny baby spends many hours asleep, we never know exactly how long it will be before he or she wakes up again. We rush round, anxiously squeezing in as many jobs as possible, in the hope that there won't be an interruption. We can't plan much, especially if we have toddlers to look after as well. As soon as we get down to a particular chore, a small person is bound to need a potty or graze a knee. And if we are having friends round for the evening, and the house is a tip, and we can hear the baby waking up again, our panic begins to mount . . .

All this can make us feel like slaves of a perpetual

cycle of demands, which pull us first one way and then the other, until it seems that we are totally consumed by our work-load. Any inward peace or prayerfulness that we might have had is likely to be smothered, because we have allowed these pressures so to dominate us that they have become a blockage between us and God.

Two ways of dealing with this situation immediately come to mind, but neither of them is satisfactory. On the one hand, we could fight against the demands, grimly rushing through them in the vain hope that, once we have got them out of the way, we will start living and praying as we would like. But this never works, and only increases our refusal to face reality.

Another danger is that we allow the chores to become a task-master, so that we simply give in, mindlessly performing one job after another. This too prevents us from coming to terms with who we are and where we are now.

There is, however, another way, which involves accepting our present situation, with all the negative and positive emotions that it arouses in us. We are *bound* to feel harassed and tired, because we are confronted by one demand after another, and often several things at once. We are *bound* to feel that we have very little independence. All this is part of being the person God has created us to be, in the place where he has put us at the moment. Our spirits can become lighter if we are able *freely to choose the inevitable*; in other words, we can find inner peace when we consciously choose to live the life which is given to us now, instead of constantly wishing that things were different.

This is not to say that we shouldn't express our

frustrations or let off steam. Of course we should. Bottling things up never helps. Nor does accepting our situation mean that we should deny ourselves treats and evenings out. That would be to succumb to an unnecessary imprisonment at home. But if we can accept the minuses as well as the pluses of everyday life, we may become free *both* from furious resentment at our lot, *and* from crawling miserably through our tasks. As Bishop Kallistos Ware observes, 'Time is the setting that makes it possible for us to choose love. Time is the interval between God's appeal and our answer.'[1]

None of us is asked to carry tomorrow's burdens as well as today's. All we have is the present moment, which is a world of its own, and this is where our energy is needed. Even if we are holding one child on our hip, listening to another, and helping an older one to clear up some black polish off the floor after an over-zealous shoe-cleaning session, we can still find a surprising sense of wholeness in our response to the situation if we give our full attention to what is happening, moment by moment.

Blow Brother Lawrence! Bless Brother Lawrence!

Surprisingly, one person who has helped me to understand this was never a parent himself. He is Brother Lawrence, a French Carmelite monk of the seventeenth century, who managed to spend his whole life walking in God's presence. He used to pray in the middle of the kitchen pots, even though he loathed washing up:

'He was never hasty nor loitering, but did each

thing in its season, with an even, uninterrupted composure and tranquillity of spirit. "The time of business," said he, "does not with me differ from the time of prayer, and in the noise and clatter of my kitchen, while several persons are at the same time calling for different things, I possess God in as great tranquillity as if I were upon my knees at the Blessed Sacrament.'"[2]

'That's all very well!' is my first reaction to that. 'But he didn't have three children, a puppy, eight stick-insects, a baby to bath, a Brownie uniform to iron, and small people "helping" to make chocolate cookies in *his* kitchen!'

Such outbursts of self-pity can, fortunately, become springboards into prayer, because it is when we have given our honest feelings to God that we can move on and face our present situation with him, clamour, headaches and all. The advice 'Protest and say Yes,' can apply to many situations, including this one.[3] We are not advocating a sugary piety, in which we murmur, 'Dear Lord, I thank you that I shall grow in patience because the children have diarrhoea and the washing machine has broken down!' We must be real with God, because then he can help us to give all our attention to whatever activity he is asking of us.

No matter how trapped we feel by household duties, our inner self remains as free as a bird; nothing can stop our spirit from soaring up to God at any moment. Christians who have faced gaol-sentences can help us to look at our own domestic 'padlocks' in this light. In her book *A Prisoner and Yet*, Corrie ten Boom writes of her time of solitary confinement:

'Outside the sun was shining. A bird was singing ... Through my window I could see gold-tipped clouds. And my fancy took flight. I saw the wide sea, the white-capped waves ... I was alone within the close confines of my cell,

but outside of my cell was the great prison, and outside of that the great wide world ... And in that world were people who were thinking about us ... It was dark in my cell. I talked with my Saviour. Never before had fellowship with him been so close. It was a joy I hoped would continue unchanged. I was a prisoner – and yet ... how free!'[4]

We are all imprisoned in some way or other. Yet, as Corrie discovered, we can all find an inner freedom in spite of our external circumstances. Some of the most physically restricted people in the world, whether through illness or hardship, have the freest spirits. Terry Waite, who was the Archbishop of Canterbury's special envoy, and spent five years as a hostage in Lebanon, is one such example in our own time. Even though he was kept in chains for most of his captivity, he never lost his faith, integrity or humour. This paradox demonstrates that we can be chained to the chores at one level, but still remain inwardly free to bring everything we do and are to God.

One moment in which we might get a taste of that freedom is when we are feeding the baby in the middle of the night. This wouldn't work for everyone, because some people never fully wake up and are far too dopey to think about anything! But for others this is a time when we can find a special peace with God, unhindered by the noises and activities of daytime. It also helps to know that some monks and nuns get up specifically to pray at night, so that they can hold the world before God while most people are asleep. We have a special bond with them at 2 a.m.!

Feeding babies at other times can be prayerful

too. The baby is plugged in, so we can't move or rush round being busy. Yet the very fact of being restricted in our movements *frees* us to give a bit more of our attention to God.

What's coming next?

Because life with toddlers and babies is unpredictable, we often have to abandon one task in order to deal with a fresh demand. Our frustration at leaving dishes half-washed or a lawn half-mown can be transformed into a 'Yes' to God, as long as we are able to let go of what we are doing and concentrate on the next thing. God is with us wherever we happen to be, and it helps if we can get away from the idea of praying *in spite of* our children, and see prayer instead as starting *in the middle of* life with them. The kingdom of God is not miles away, but in our midst, as Jesus himself reminds us (Luke 17:21).

Haste – necessary or not?

When six tasks need doing and we only have half an hour, we will almost certainly be in such a rush that our sense of 'surrender to God' will be minimal. It is always difficult to be in conscious communion with God when we are in a hurry. If we do manage anything in God's direction, it will probably be no more than a gasp of thanks or a prayer for help to keep going. And we shouldn't feel guilty if that is the case. At such times I like to use the well-known prayer: 'Lord, you know how busy I must be today. If I forget you, please don't forget me.'[5]

Sometimes haste is unavoidable. But hurrying can become a habit if we are not careful. Constantly racing against time destroys our inner peace; our thoughts about future jobs race and tumble over each other, so that we leave no space within ourselves for God, or for the gifts he is offering us in the present moment. It is a useful exercise to notice how many times in a day we rush unnecessarily. Perpetual speed may save us five or ten minutes a day. But at what cost?

Meister Eckhart, the fourteenth century German mystic, wrote, 'Wisdom consists in doing the next thing you have to do, doing it with your whole heart, and finding delight in doing it.'[6] There are many ways in which whole-hearted attention opens up a way to prayer. The moment when our children triumphantly bring home their art and handwork is one example. It makes all the difference if we can drop what we are doing and look at their treasures carefully. Rushing the process not only hurts our children, but also denies us the pleasure of being absorbed with them and looking contemplatively at their pictures. If we can make space in ourselves to ponder the colours, shapes and designs in front of us, this leads naturally into gratitude to God for our children and for their creative gifts. Then the serious business of choosing which pictures to stick on the kitchen wall will provide us with material for thanksgiving for months to come.

Another example of the benefit which comes from 'doing what we are doing' is when we take the family out to the beach or the country. If we only play games with them half-heartedly, or try to read the paper and supervise their playing at the same time, we may well spoil their enjoyment as well as our own. Whole-hearted participation on our own part will enable us to receive the happiness that God is offering us at this moment.

Joy in heaven

The story of Jesus welcoming some children while the disciples fussed and tried to shoo them away, is so familiar that we easily miss the bubbling joy in this episode (Mark 10:13–14). (The archaic word '*Suffer* the little children . . .' in the old translation doesn't help!)

I cannot believe that Jesus was resigning himself to being with the children as a tiresome duty, or that he perched them stiffly on his knee for a strictly limited period, as though they were an interruption of his *real* work! I suspect that he *wanted* to hold them close and have fun with them, and play games and be ridiculous with them, because being with children invigorated him and gave him a special sense of the divine love and joy. 'Let the children come to me,' he said, 'and do not stop them, because the kingdom of God belongs to such as these' (Mark 10:14 GNB). Playing keeps us human – *and* close to the spirit of Jesus.

In the next two chapters I explore more fully some practical ways in which we can pray in the middle of everyday life. But if you are weighed down with weariness and low spirits, you may wish to turn straight to Chapter 5.

* * *

Lord, the next time I find myself thinking, 'I'm only playing with the children,' or 'I'm only sorting the washing,' help me to stop saying 'only'. Even when I'm tired, help me to surrender my activity to you, so that I can give myself fully to what needs doing. Let me remember that this is your will for me, here and now, and show me how to receive the good things and the gladness that you offer me.

*Self abandonment to the present moment
is not easy.*

CHAPTER 3

Attentiveness

Keep your heart with all vigilance;
for from it flows the springs of life.
Let your eyes look directly forward,
and your gaze be straight before you.
(Proverbs 4:23, 25)

As busy people, we can easily go through our days
neither seeing nor hearing the things around us,
because we are so preoccupied with our own thoughts
and concerns. One result is that our prayer suffers,
since the endless, habitual chatter in our minds
crowds out our communion with God, as well as
our awareness of the world in general. But it is we
who are cutting ourselves off from God and not vice
versa. He is constantly making himself known to us
through the gifts in his creation, if we will only look
and listen.

If we can, therefore, begin to let go of the incessant
monologue in our brains, and become more inwardly
open and receptive, we will find all sorts of richness
in everyday life that we had not noticed before. Our
children can teach us something here. They love
to touch, feel and taste things, and instinctively

investigate whatever is under their noses, from the baby who puts everything into his mouth to the three-year-old who sticks her finger into every dish in the kitchen. They know how to delight in things, while the world floats past us adults and we miss it!

Harassed parents often remark, 'It's always NOW with the kids! They can't wait for anything!' This is true, and can be exasperating. But our children's capacity to live in the present has a positive side to it as well. Take a typical tea-time. The table is set, the food is ready. The baby is in her high chair, and you have called the older children in from the garden. But instead of coming and sitting down straight away at the table, they crowd excitedly into the kitchen and want to show you some ladybirds which they have collected.

What do you do? The temptation is to ignore their enthusiasm and grumble about the tea getting cold. But, if you do that, you risk smothering their joy. After all, which is more important? Serving a perfect tea, or spending a few minutes with the ladybirds? Why not feed the baby while the others show you their findings? *Let* the scrambled egg get cold! Relax!

'I bless you, Father,' says Jesus in Luke 10, 'for hiding these things from the learned and the clever, and revealing them to children' (v. 21 JB).

One of my favourite books as a child consisted of a long picture, folded like a concertina. It began with a footpath in the country, and gradually developed into a farmyard track, then a lane, then a side-road, then a B-road and finally a main road leading into a city. I used to find endless pleasure in the wealth of colourful details at each stage of the way. Although the book's climax was the grand-looking city at the end, every part of the journey was of equal value to me. Now that I am a distracted adult the magic of this book has come alive for me again, especially with the help of my children, who are so good at discovering buried treasure in ordinary moments.

Too busy to notice?
All five of our senses can be doorways into prayer, if we use them attentively, because the earth is shot through with the goodness of God: 'In the beginning, God created heaven and earth. And God saw, and behold it was very good' (Genesis 1:31). But if we are so busy that we brush past life, lost in our own reveries, we are liable to forget that everything we use, handle and enjoy is a gift from God. It is worth trying to increase our awareness, so that we truly see what we are looking at, feel what we are holding and taste what we are eating. This enables life's daily ingredients to lead us into prayer, so that we become more thankful to God and meet him in and through the things he has made.

Look at the objects which fill our homes: furniture, gadgets, food, ornaments, books, toys, etc. Each one, from a tomato to an electric drill, is a product of God's creative energy combined with human activity, and each has been entrusted to us. We can feel its weight, texture and design, ponder its colour, and pray for our fellow human beings who contributed to its arrival in our home. Attentiveness of this sort is not just a clever technique to make us into alert people. We are deliberately using our physical senses as triggers to sharpen our awareness of God's goodness, and to hear his challenge to us in the world.

Your own sign of God's presence

Perhaps there is an object that you often use or look at, which could become a reminder of God's love for you. A friend of mine found that something as odd as a skating-boot became a sign of God's care for her; a bad relationship had been healed at her skating club, and she now wanted to thank God for this, and for the exhilaration of movement on the ice. So she used her boot as a focus for this prayer, and hung it on her bedroom wall, next to a cross.

Someone else finds a prayerful moment when she puts on her spectacles in the morning, and can suddenly see clearly. All sorts of prayers could arise from so simple an action, e.g., 'Thank you Lord for my sight,' or 'Open my eyes to the needs of your world today.' Another person once wrote in a letter: 'I was looking at the pencil in my hand, and thinking about the wood which surrounds the lead. I thought to myself, "This thin piece of lead wouldn't be much use without the strong wood to hold it. Yet people only seem to be interested in the marks made by the lead, and not in the wood that supports it. So the wood has a hidden role, without which the pencil's drawing and writing would never be possible." And I wondered if God was asking me to have a hidden ministry too. I can't do much, or make my mark on the world. But I can support other people by my concern and prayer. It was good to realise that this praying of mine is as important to God's work as the wood is to the pencil lead!'

We need to wait and see what signs of his love and wisdom God may be offering us. We cannot force this. It's no good scouring the shelves and trying to squeeze some spiritual meaning out of a can of oil or a tin of pilchards. What is required is that we keep awake and alert, like the servants waiting for their master in Jesus' parable (Luke 12:35–40), so that we are ready for whatever God may give us.

When a friend presents us with a gift, we receive something of that person, as well as the particular object they are giving to us. Similarly, if we spend time with an artist and look at his or her work intently and appreciatively, our relationship with them will deepen in the process. The same kind of thing happens between us and God when we are attentive to his world.[1] He gives us something of himself through what he has made, if we are open enough to receive him.

Most of us find it hard to be aware of all five senses at once. So it helps to concentrate on one particular sense for a period of perhaps one day, and then move on to another sense when we feel ready. This chapter includes specific suggestions about praying with sight, hearing, touch, taste and smell (see pages 48, 50, 54 and 57).

Feel your feet!
One way of using touch as prayer is to feel our feet. (By this I mean being aware of the sensations in our feet, rather than grabbing hold of a foot!) This brings our awareness back to where we are at this moment, and *this* is where God is. Even though there are likely to be several layers of material and substance between our feet and the soil, this is still a useful reminder that we are children of the earth, and dependent on its Creator for our existence. We can pray in this way at any time – when walking in the park or working in the kitchen, sitting in a traffic-jam or standing in a queue. If we persevere,

we may discover, as Jacob did, that everywhere is holy ground:

'Surely the Lord is in this place, and I did not know it ... This is none other than the house of God.' (Genesis 28: 16–17)

TOUCHING

(You might like to add your own ideas)

- feel my feet
- enjoy washing and drying my hands
- notice the texture of things I handle, letting this become thanksgiving, e.g. clothes, wood, plastic, glass etc.
- try not to snatch or grasp anything
- make the preparing of food into an act of celebration, even when time is limited
- pray for the children through the way I touch them (n.b. how do I grab hold of them when I'm in a hurry?)
- receive God's love for me as the world touches me

God said to Moses on Mount Horeb, 'Put off your shoes from your feet, for the place on which you are standing is holy ground.' (Exodus 3:8)

A leper came to Jesus and knelt before him saying, 'Lord, if you will, you can make me clean.' And he stretched out his hand and touched him.' (Matthew 8: 2–3)

Sight and prayer

In his picture *Fool and Butterfly*, Cecil Collins has created a profound sense of reverence and stillness. The Fool, who looks child-like and almost comical at first, gazes in rapt attention at a creature which is more like a dragonfly than a butterfly. To Collins,

LOOKING

– take time to see the expression on my children's faces; have another look at the colour of their eyes

– enjoy some of my favourite pictures on the walls

– take a clear and steady look at the trees near my home

– look carefully at the children's models and paintings

– when I cut through fruit and vegetables, pause to look at their colour and structure

Jesus said, 'Consider the lilies of the field, how they grow; they neither toil nor spin; yet even Solomon in all his glory was not arrayed like one of these.' (Matthew 6:28–29)

(At Emmaus) When Jesus was at table with them, he took the bread and blessed and broke it, and gave it to them. And their eyes were opened and they recognised him. (Luke 24:30–31)

Blessed are the pure in heart, for they shall see God. (Matthew 5:8)

the figure of the Fool represents a clear and pure vision of life; the Fool is as free from worldy power and status as a child, and his outlook is unspoilt by cynicism (see page 49).

In this painting, light reflects from the face and hands of the Fool, and also from the face of the butterfly which gazes back at him. The attitude of our own faces and hands towards the world will determine whether we, like the Fool, are capable of receiving and reflecting its God-given glory. Nowadays it is our young people who are the most aware of the urgent need to cherish this planet, and the rest of us need to learn from them. It has been aptly said, 'If you want to know the truth, ask a child or a fool.'[2]

Both the fir-cone and the butterfly in Collins's painting are traditional symbols of resurrection. This too is food for thought, because when we open up our senses to 'see and perceive, hear and understand' (Mark 4:12), we move out of our spiritual deadness into a new and richer life with God in his world. There is so much beauty around us, in everyday things like spiders' webs, or the brightly coloured patterns on the family's clothes. Children have no difficulty enjoying conkers, kittens and carnivals; let's follow their example!

> Earth's crammed with heaven,
> And every common bush afire with God.
> But only he who sees takes off his shoes;
> The rest sit round it and pluck blackberries.
> (Elizabeth Barrett-Browning)[3]

Realities beneath the surface

Jesus was so utterly open to God and the world that he couldn't help seeing the truths of the kingdom in everything, from a loaf of bread to a coin on the floor (Luke 13: 21, 15: 8–10). He had what could be called a 'sacramental' way of observing life, because he constantly perceived an inner significance in outward things, especially in the down-to-earth matters of fields, families and households.

Our children, too, find it easy to see hidden realities beneath outward appearances. 'That's a space-station,' announced my small daughter one day, pointing proudly to a collection of foil pie-dishes, lumps of Plasticine and hair-grips. 'And that's the astronauts' coffee-machine!' added her younger brother as he stuck an old magnet into the middle. So this little heap of objects, which meant nothing to the uninitiated, took its place of honour on the side-board as a space-station, and sparked off in me a great deal of thanksgiving for my children and their lively imagination.

So our lives can become more prayerful if we develop the same capacity to see as our children have. In her book *A Tree Full of Angels*, Macrina Wiederkehr writes,

'The incredible gift of the ordinary! Glory comes streaming from the table of daily life. Will I be there to catch the rays, or will I remain blind to the holy because I'm too busy to see? Am I too busy with my own agenda to let God's agenda bless me? . . . O God deliver me from shallow living!'[4]

The trouble is that most of us are forgetful creatures, so it can help to put small signs or pictures around the house, such as icons and prayer-cards, to remind us that God is here. These prayer-cards, for instance,[5] placed on a wall or mantlepiece, can become like places of 'pilgrims' rest' where we can stop briefly, be refreshed, and rekindle our sense of God's presence.

LISTENING

– listen to the birds, especially first thing in the morning, and when walking along the street

– be aware of all the sounds around me

– let go of mental chatter every time I become aware of it

– pay attention to what people are saying to me, both through their words and their gestures

– try to listen to music without thoughts rattling through my brain at the same time

– notice – am I a noisy person?

Be still and know that I am God. (Psalm 46:10)

Morning by morning God wakens my ear, to listen as one who is taught. (Isaiah 50: 4–5)

Earthiness and wonder

Giving our full attention to whatever situation we are in can affect the way we look at all kinds of mundane occupations, even things as basic as nappy-changing. Every parent will have discovered the scope for fun and delight in this task, when our baby relishes the chance to kick vigorously in the air without encumbrance, and rewards us with that radiant, toothless smile! But there is more. Lying on the mat in front of us is one of the wonders of human existence – a digestive system! Our bodies are far cleverer than we are in the way this function is performed. Even the greatest expert on human anatomy depended on his body to dispose of waste-products efficiently, before he could even walk or talk. Right in the middle of her classic teaching on the spiritual life, Julian of Norwich meditates on this in a delightful passage:

'A man goes upright
and the food of his body is sealed as in a purse full fair;
and when it is time of his necessity, it is opened
and sealed again full honestly.'

She goes on from this to observe:

'Our Lord comes down to us to the lowest part of our need.
for he does not despise what he has created.'
(*Revelations of the Divine Love* Chapter 6.)[6]

All of life can be a gateway into prayer if we will only wake up. The whisper of God's gentleness, the touch of his warmth, the taste of his goodness, the scent of his holiness and the glimpse of his glory, are all offered to us in our daily living. Will we allow each day to teach us?

Prayer of a Teapot

God, you created me
and I am glad;
glad too that I can warm people's hearts
and create home and fellowship.

I am old now and ugly and battered;
made of dull pottery
with a broken, stained spout
and a cracked lid.
But I have some pride in myself.
I've a good handle
round which fingers curl snugly and confidently.
I pour well too.

Much of the day I sit on the dresser
with bigger and smaller teapots
all in better shape than I.
I really come to life only when I'm used;
when someone warms me up
and I feel the tea fall into me
and the boiling water quickly fills me.
Then I warm through and,
as I sit on the table,
smiling and drawing everyone to me,
I feel, God, that you created me to be used.
I feel needed and valued
and at the heart of community,
of people who are relaxing,
laughing and talking round the kitchen table;
or of people who are in pain and anguish,
suffering from the shock of bad news.

Use me again and again
that I may know I am alive.
(J. de Rooy S.J.)[7]

TASTING and SMELLING

   – don't gulp down food without noticing what I am eating; relish the various flavours
   – don't eat and do jobs at the same time
   – stop to enjoy the scent of flowers, shrubs and herbs in the house and garden
   – enjoy smelling the baby's hair
   – give thanks for the aromas from the kitchen when baking
   – enjoy the smell outside after rain

As Jesus sat at table in his house, . . . the scribes and the Pharisees said, 'Why does he eat and drink with tax collectors and sinners? . . . Behold, a glutton and a drunkard!' (Matthew 9: 10–11; 11:19)

> *I come to my garden, my sister, my bride,*
> *I gather my myrrh with my spice,*
> *I eat my honeycomb with my honey,*
> *I drink my wine with my milk.*
> *Eat, O friends, and drink: drink deeply, O lovers! (Song of Solomon 5:1)*

Mary took a pound of costly ointment of pure nard and anointed the feet of Jesus and wiped his feet with her hair; and the house was filled with the fragrance of the ointment. (John 12:3)

A SPACE FOR STILLNESS

Before you start . . . see page 30.

Ψ Read the sections *Too busy to Notice?* and *Your Own Sign of God's Presence* (pages 45 and 46). Take an everyday object that you have used or looked at recently. Look at it carefully. Thank God for its substance, usefulness or beauty, and the skill that has made it. Think about its texture, shape and colour. See if God is saying anything to you through this object, but don't force anything! It may be enough simply to enjoy it with God.

Ψ Read the *Prayer of a Teapot* (pages 55 and 56). Do you relate to the teapot's experience? Remember that you are special to God, just as you are. Allow his love to fill you and warm you from the inside. Ask God to use you to bless others.

Ψ Read slowly through the page on TOUCHING (page 48). Chew over the verses from Scripture on this page. Offer to God your intention to use your sense of touch as a way into prayer during your everyday activity.

Ψ Do the same with LOOKING (page 50).

Ψ Do the same with LISTENING (page 54).

Ψ Do the same with TASTING AND SMELLING (page 57).

Ψ Read the section *Feel your feet* on pages 47 and 48. Relax your whole body, bit by bit, starting from the top of your head and moving slowly down to your feet. Think about the sensations in each part as you move downwards. When you are thinking about your mouth, chin and neck, offer to God all your speaking; with your arms and hands offer him all your physical work, and so on. When you reach your feet, feel their pressure on the ground and use this prayer:

Lord, Creator of the world,
I thank you for making me,
in a mysterious dependence
on the rhythms and fruits
of your earth.
Let me be wholly present to you,
here,
where my feet are on the ground,
now.

Ψ Spend time with the picture *Fool and Butterfly* (page 49), and read the thoughts about it on pages 50 and 51. Ask God to speak to you through this picture, so that it becomes for you an 'icon' or window into the divine love which permeates creation. You could use these words from Psalm 148, before staying quietly with the picture:

Mountains and all hills,
fruit trees and all cedars!
Beasts and all cattle,
creeping things and flying birds!
Young men and maidens together,
old men and children!
Let them praise the name of the Lord;
for he commanded and they were created.
(from vv. 9–13)

*Sorry Lord! You know that I **do** want to celebrate your birth.*

CHAPTER 4

Thread-words

Let the word of Christ dwell in you richly. Let the peace of Christ rule in your hearts. (Colossians 3: 15, 16)

During the weeks leading up to Christmas some years ago, I was almost overwhelmed by the number of special events and extra tasks which had to be fitted in. I wasn't well, I was sleeping badly, and I became increasingly jaded and irritable. What kept my spiritual life going during that difficult time was a prayer which I said over and over again under my breath: 'Jesus, have mercy on me; Jesus, live in me'. These words calmed me and brought me back to Jesus' ever-present help and forgiveness. Constantly repeating the prayer gave some coherence to the fragmented jumble of activities that I was squeezing into each day.

In the past I used to call short prayers like this 'word-friends'[1], because they are good companions when life is hectic. But I now call them 'thread-words', because they hold my life together like a thread, and help to keep me centred on God.

There are many different ways of choosing a thread-word. You may have a moment over an early-morning cup of tea, when you can consider what word or phrase to take with you for the day. A verse from Scripture or a sentence in a book may strike you, or you may want to go back to a prayer you have often used before. A notebook for jotting down favourite texts can be a useful resource to consult quickly when there is no time to stop and think.

Some Christians are cautious about using prayers over and over again, because it seems like the 'vain repetition' against which Jesus warned us (Matthew 6:7)[2]. But using 'thread-words' is quite different, because we are making an act of heart and will, and expressing our desire to have God at the centre of our lives. We are living and breathing words of God's love and wisdom, in the trust that they will become woven into the fabric of our lives as his constant gift to us.

Suppose you choose a prayer based on Paul's words in Colossians 3:3: 'Let me be hidden with Christ in God'. If you repeat this often enough, it will take root in you, so that you become increasingly aware of Christ's love flowing through your consciousness. This should have an effect on the way you cope with the day's events. If, for example, you find a newly cleaned room reduced to a sea of sticky confusion, or if someone at work lets you down, your thread-word will be there to return to, and will help to keep you close to Christ, come what may.

An imaginary monologue

'Christmas Eve tomorrow! Amy woke up covered in spots – it's chicken-pox, so she can't be the Angel Gabriel in the church play, poor kid. This evening some of the family drove the twelve miles to the bus station to meet Grandma, who is staying for

Christmas. The car broke down on the way. She got so cold waiting for them that she eventually found a taxi, and arrived here none too pleased. The others came back at midnight, and we were all rather bad-tempered.

Jesus, have mercy on me; Jesus, live in me.

The drains are blocked up; I spent two fruitless hours trying to clear them this afternoon, when I should have been wrapping presents. Nobody will be able to have a bath until we can find someone to come and fix them after Christmas. To crown it all, the hamster escaped while the younger ones were cleaning out his cage, and the cat got him.

Jesus, have mercy on me; Jesus, live in me.

Who says Christmas is merry? Sorry, Lord! You know that I do want to celebrate your birth. Yet it's so difficult with all this chaos going on. And I feel guilty that I'm sorry for myself, when thousands are starving and homeless while we have so much. But thank you, Lord, with all my heart, for everything that Christmas means.

Jesus, have mercy on me; Jesus, live in me.'

Words as channels of love – ours for God, and his for us

Words are remarkable things. They are infinitely more than lines and dots on a page, or vibrations of sound in the air – though that is what they are at one level. Words point to a reality beyond themselves. For instance, the words 'I love you,' consisting of eight letters, three consonants and five vowels, point to the reality of 'love' which is far greater than any words. They are simply the channel or instrument for conveying that love. The same is true when we use verbal prayers. We often need to talk to God to express our love and need of him; but the love itself transcends any words, and we sometimes end up simply being there with God in a loving and prayerful silence. And even if we don't *feel* as if we love God much, the very act of using a phrase such as 'Lord, you know that I love you' (John 21: 15) can make our love more of a reality.

Breathing as prayer

Praying as we breathe is a good way of taking into ourselves the life and love of God, just as, in the Genesis story, God breathed life into Adam, whose name means 'humankind' (Genesis 2: 7). Breathing-prayer works well with a name such as 'Jesus' or 'Lord', or a noun like 'love,' 'mercy' or 'peace'. A prayer which fits well with the rhythm of breathing while we walk along is: *'Christ, my Lord; Christ, my Light,'* or simply, *'Christ, Lord; Christ, Light.'* You may like to take several breaths after each word, as a way of absorbing its impact more deeply. Some people say the words with their 'in' breaths, others with their 'out' breaths. Whatever pattern you find best, breathing with a thread-word is another way of 'abiding in Christ' during both the predictable and the unexpected moments.

Beads on a thread

On some necklaces all the beads are the same, while others have beads of different shapes, sizes and colours. Similarly, when we are praying with thread-words, we may want to use an identical phrase for some time, or we may prefer to change our prayer more often.

On pages 65 to 68 there are some threads of 'beads' containing short verses, prayers and thoughts which

Light

Light of Christ, shine on me,
Light of Christ, shine through me.

The light shines in the darkness,
And the darkness has not overcome it.
(John 1:5)

Christ is the morning star,
who brings the promise of the light of life,
and opens everlasting day.
(The Ven. Bede)

Make me
a still place
of light.

Arise, shine, for your light has come,
and the glory of the Lord has risen upon you.
(Isaiah 60:1)

God doesn't solve our pain,
but, in Jesus,
he chooses to share our dark,
to live through it with us,
and, by so doing, transform it.
(Dr. Margaret Spufford)[3]

Lord, let me be open to your light,
soaked in your light,
and transparent with your light.

Water

As a deer longs for flowing streams,
so longs my soul for you,
O God. (Psalm 42:1 NRSV)

"I will pour water
on the thirsty land,
and streams
on the dry ground,"
says the Lord.
(Isaiah 44:3)

Living water of Christ,
cleanse and purify me,
and be a spring of eternal life
welling up within me.

Let me trust in God,
'like a tree planted by water,
that sends out its roots by the stream,
and does not fear when heat comes.'
(Jeremiah. 17:8)

Lord, may your peaceful presence
be like a well of still, clear water
within me.

Lord, you are my lover,
my longing,
My flowing stream,
my sin,
and I
am your reflection.
(Mechtilde of Magdeburg, 13th Century)[4]

Rest

Lord, you made me for yourself,
and my heart is restless
until it finds rest in you.
(St. Augustine)

Jesus said, 'Come to me,
all who labour and are heavy laden,
and I will give you rest.'
(Matt. 11:28)

Lord, however busy I am,
help me to rest inwardly in you.

'In returning and in rest
you shall be saved,
In quietness and in trust
shall be your strength.'
(Isaiah 30:15)

'The place of rest
is being loved by God.'

I smiled to think
God's greatness
flowed round our incompleteness;
round our restlessness
his rest.
(Elizabeth Barrett-Browning)[6]

I will lie down in peace
and take my rest,
For you alone, O Lord,
make me dwell in safety.
(from Psalm 4:8)

Fire

Lord, let the flame of your love
kindle my whole heart,
may I burn towards you,
wholly love you, set aflame by you.
(St. Augustine)

'The angel of the Lord appeared to Moses
in a flame of fire out of the midst
of a bush; . . . and the bush was burning,
yet it was not consumed.' (Exod. 3:2)

Holy Spirit,
Light and fire of love,
baptise me, transform me,
and burn away the selfishness in me.

Lord, let all my loving be part of the fire
which you came to cast on the earth.
(cf. Luke 12:49)

Fire is kindled
when God's self-emptying in Christ
meets our self-emptying in prayer.
(St. Isaac the Syrian, 7th century)

Set our hearts on fire
with love for you, O Christ,
that, in its flame, we may love you
with all our heart and mind
and soul and strength,
and bring warmth and comfort
to our neighbours.
(based on an Eastern Orthodox prayer)[7]

can be used in whatever way is right for you. A single bead may give you enough nourishment to keep you going for a while. Or you may want to move on to a new one as soon as the next opportunity arises. Take as long or as short a time as you wish over each bead, letting its theme flow through all the activities of your day. It doesn't matter that you will often forget the thread-word in the middle of your busyness. The words are there, in your subconscious, for you to come back to again and again.

Having used the suggestions in this book, you might like to make your own threads of beads, asking God to guide you in this: 'Let my life be underpinned by prayer; let prayer be the thread that holds me together.'

Words lead to stillness

There is stillness beneath every sound, and all noises and words are imposed upon the silence, like pictures set against a white background. Inside ourselves, too, there is a still centre underneath our chattering consciousness. Gently repeating thread-words is one way in which we can enter that inner pool of quietness, especially if we are able to be alone for a few minutes.

The Psalmist advises us to 'commune in our own hearts and be still' (Psalm 4:4). But he recommends that we do it on our beds! As busy people we will probably find other places more appropriate for dipping into the silence, like the ironing board or the garden. Finding inner peace is not an automatic process, and there will be times when we feel that contemplative or wordless prayer is out of our reach. But it's worth persevering in the attempt to root our hectic existence in the stillness of God.

There is a remarkable verse in Isaiah 30:15, which can help us in this.

In returning and in rest you shall be saved.
In quietness and trust shall be your strength.[8]

There are two pairs of ideas here, in the parallel pattern often found in Hebrew poetry:

RETURN + REST:
QUIETNESS + TRUST.

These four words alone make a useful thread-word, especially on an impossible day, even though it may seem crazy to take words like 'rest' and 'quiet' when we are surrounded by noisy chaos. But the words help us to remember that God is always offering us his tranquil love, even when there's a gas meter-reader at the front door, a child sitting on a potty and a pan of unstirred custard rapidly turning into lumps on the cooker.

Return. This is the heart of the Gospel. God gently draws us back, again and again, to turn our faces and hearts towards him. The Hebrew words for 'turning' and 'repentance' in the Old Testament are the same, and God never denies us the chance to turn ourselves round and re-align our wills with his. Conversion is an on-going process.

Rest. When we are worn out and near to our wits' end, God offers us his rest. He invites us to pour our inner tension and turmoil into him, and to become passive in his arms for a few moments. When we rest in God like this 'our poverty meets his giving in the silence of lovers.'[9] Isaiah surprises us by teaching that it is in this rest, rather than in our own frantic efforts, that we shall be saved.

Quietness. This is crucial to our relationship with God. In a world obsessed with productivity and results, it may seem strange to regard quietness as a source of strength. In the church we often assume that Christians should be armed to the teeth with ideas, arguments and plans. Yet we must have quietness, in order to be hollowed out before God, and to give space for his grace to work in and through us. And when we are surrounded by crying children, clamouring clients or urgent jobs, we can draw strength from the fact that we have dipped into God's stillness, even if only for a fleeting moment.

Trust. This is based, not on compulsion, but on freedom. Trust means stepping out with God into the unknown territory of every day, surrendering ourselves and the people we love into his hands, and entrusting to him the outcome of everything we do.

Return – Rest – Quietness – Trust

Using these words is not a way of escaping from dreary chores into a pious dream-world. On the contrary, the words guide and purify us, so that we are enabled to live a bit more 'in Christ' wherever we are and whatever we are doing.

O Christ,
serene and tranquil Light,
shine into the depth of my being,
come, and draw me to yourself.
Free me from the chatter of my mind,
and draw me through and beyond
the words and symbols
into the silence,

that I may discover you,
the unspoken Word,
beyond all words,
the pure Light
piercing and transforming the darkness
that veils the ground of my being.[5]

A SPACE FOR STILLNESS

Before you start . . . *see page* 30

●Read the first section of Chapter 4 (pages 61 and 62). Choose a thread-word and let it lead you into quietness with God.

●Read the section *Breathing as Prayer* (page 64) As you remain still and quiet, use a thread-word with the rhythm of your breathing.

●Read the section *Words lead to stillness* (pages 69 to 71) Spend time with the verse from Isaiah 30:15, 'In returning and in rest . . .' You might prefer to stay with the single word 'Return' today, and move on to the word 'Rest' next time you have a space, and so on.

●Say the prayer on page 72 slowly and thoughtfully. Let Christ's light and warmth penetrate you.

They don't discipline their children
these days!

CHAPTER 5

When We Feel Inadequate

Out of the depths I cry to you, O Lord. Lord, hear my voice. (Psalm 130:1 NRSV)

Most of us feel low and weary at some point in our lives. Women are particularly vulnerable to 'the blues' after a baby is born, although patches of depression can occur as the children grow older too. Anybody, whether father or mother, parent or non-parent, can become depressed, and praying is not easy when our spirits are down.

The very nature of depression seems to militate against prayerfulness, because you are in a no-win situation. You long to be comforted, yet you don't want to face other people. You feel you can't cope with your work, yet you find offers of help difficult because they make you feel incompetent. You desperately want to be affirmed as a parent, and fret over the slightest criticism; yet the very fact that you do this can easily irritate others! To make matters worse, you can feel guilty because you believe that you *ought* to be grateful to have children, yet you are so weary that you simply want to curl up in a corner and sink into oblivion.

We would hardly choose a state like this as a

setting for prayer! Yet there is hope. For the more we realise how badly we need God, the closer we are to him – even though it may not seem so at the time.

Love Unlimited

A certain incident in Jesus's life can be a source of reassurance when we think that our spiritual life has reached an all-time low. Simon the Pharisee had invited Jesus for a meal, and a woman with a doubtful reputation, whose life had clearly hit rock bottom, came into the place where they were eating (Luke 7:36–50). Jesus had probably given her a sense of her own value, in a way which nobody had ever done before. So she now approached Jesus, washed his feet with her tears, dried them with her hair and anointed them with oil. The Pharisee was filled with righteous indignation at this and blamed Jesus for letting such a woman touch him. Reading Simon's thoughts, Jesus responded, 'Her sins, which are many, are forgiven, for she loved much' (verse 47).

No matter how wretched or worthless you feel, Jesus loves you just as he loved that woman. You could try making Jesus's reply to her into words spoken directly to you: 'Your sins are forgiven, for you have loved much.' Christ's love does not have to be earned; it is offered to us all the time, as a free gift. This is the miracle of the Gospel.

In spite of all your attempts to receive Christ's love, you may still be enveloped in a cloud of guilt, feeling that you can't summon the energy to think about Jesus at all, because it's taking all your strength to drag yourself through the day's immediate tasks. In that case a different approach to praying might be more helpful.

Draw life from your baby

Your baby draws life from you, not only through having been procreated by you and lived in the womb for nine months, but also because you now seem to be pouring out your very existence in order to keep her (or him) fed, clean, sheltered and loved. We easily forget that this small, dependent creature is also a potential source of energy and warmth *for us*. We have become so embroiled in the domestic routine surrounding her life, that we forget to receive the gifts she can offer us. So try praying with your baby, letting God use her to pour strength into you. Hold her close, smell her hair, touch her skin, listen to her breathing. Reflect on the miracle of how God's life-giving power created her, a tiny new part of humankind, and let that energy flow through you as well. Ponder the words

> 'God's life in you; God's life in me.
> God's love in you, God's love in me.'

Two-way arrows

If we are at a low ebb, the 'thread-words' that I describe earlier (in Chapter 4) may become absolutely crucial in our struggle to hang on to God. These short prayers are like arrows, shot in desperation to the God whom we need but cannot find among the perpetual demands. The term 'arrow-prayers' is a well-known name for these cries to God for help. But I prefer to regard them as 'two-way arrows'. Otherwise it could seem as if we are shooting darts at a remote God in order to prick him and gain his attention. But prayer is two-way traffic. God is waiting for us to reach out to him, and when we release our arrow of need he penetrates us with his own 'dart of love'.[1]

God does respond when we cry for help, and he works to heal and bless us even if we are not aware of it at the time. We may be so swallowed up in our present darkness that we cannot feel his presence or love for us at the moment. But afterwards, on looking back, we may see that God was there, holding us, all the time.

Permission to let off steam

Things have a habit of building up! Suppose you've had no time to yourself all day, even to read your post or glance at the paper; the baby has cried incessantly, you've had a birthday party for your four-year-old, and the house is in total disarray. As you clear up and finally sit down, aching with tiredness, the door-bell rings and a neighbour comes in. She settles herself in an armchair, stares at the finger-marks on the wall and tells you how lucky you are not to have teenagers. When she eventually leaves, you are so over-wrought that you snap at the children about something trivial; instantly regretting this, you break into floods of tears.

Explode to God about it! It's all right to do so! Tell him exactly what you think of your life and the tiresome neighbour and everything else. Some people hesitate to pray like this, because it seems disrespectful to God. But if our best friend were to turn up at that moment, we would have a good moan and cry, and probably end up feeling much better, perhaps even laughing about things. God is no less approachable than our best friend!

Praying as honestly as this can be both comforting and cleansing. When we expose everything to God, including our unpleasant reactions, we are taking a crucial step towards relief, forgiveness and healing. In her wisdom, Julian of Norwich writes, 'Although we feel miseries, disputes, and strifes in ourselves, yet are we all mercifully enwrapped in the kindliness of God and in his gentleness.'[2] We come back again to the essential truth that God embraces us in his tender love, just as we would hold our child close if he or she were shaking with rage and misery.

Who am I?

Being a new parent can lead to an identity crisis. Life changes drastically and our independence is severely limited. We are so absorbed in the domestic treadmill that our brains seem to go into reverse gear. When my babies were small, I used to have difficulty remembering even the most obvious things, and it was hard to concentrate on reading anything.

To make matters worse, we begin to imagine that we no longer have a role in the world; women are particularly prone to this. It is as if the person we thought we were has got lost somewhere in the process of giving birth. This is a harsh wilderness experience, aggravated by tiredness and the lack of opportunities for peace and solitude with God.

There is something we can do in such circumstances, though it's a tough challenge: we can ask God to make our unhappiness into a stripping and purifying experience. Since we have so few resources of our own, we are thrown back on God's grace, strength and forgiveness. Our inner emptiness has put us among the 'poor in spirit', and *they* are the people whom Jesus describes as being especially blessed in God's eyes (Matt. 5:3). The fact that we are so aware of our inadequacy means that there is more room for God to work in us. This is the paradox: when we accept that we have nothing, God can become everything. One way of expressing this in prayer is to hold the palms of our hands out to God, as a sign of our total need of him.

Some meditations to use when you have a chance

Ponder these words from Deuteronomy, which describe how God deals with his people:

> He found him in a desert land,
> and in the howling waste of the wilderness;
> he encircled him, he cared for him,
> he kept him as the apple of his eye.
> Like an eagle that stirs up its nest,
> that flutters over its young,
> spreading out its wings, catching them,
> bearing them on its pinions. (Deut. 32:10–11)

Try reading this passage again slowly, and make it apply to you personally:

> He found *me* in a desert land,
> and in the howling waste of the wilderness;
> he encircled *me*, he cared for *me*,
> he kept *me* as the apple of his eye.
> Like an eagle that stirs up its nest,
> that flutters over its young,
> spreading out its wings, catching *me*,
> bearing *me* on its pinions. (Deut. 32:10–11)

Remember, you *are* valuable; you *are* God's unique and beloved child. Hear him say to you:

Do not be afraid, for I have redeemed you;
I have called you by your name, you are mine.
Should you pass through the sea, I will be with
you,
or through rivers, they will not swallow you
up.
Should you walk through fire, you will not
be scorched,
and the flames will not burn you.
Because you are precious in my eyes,
because you are honoured and I love you, says
the Lord.
(Isaiah 43: 1b, 2, 4a JB)

Be a fool for Christ

Most women find that having babies is a blow to their dignity. I don't just mean having our feet held up in stirrups while they examine us or sew us up (though that's bad enough). The knock to our pride goes much deeper. It can be unnerving suddenly to feel incompetent and weepy, especially if this is the first baby and we have been used to holding down a responsible job. Then there are numerous embarrassments, such as the patches of leaking milk on the front of a T-shirt, or the indignant looks from passers-by when we are annoyed with a toddler in public. Things can slip uncomfortably out of control in all sorts of ways.

Take a visit to the shops on a hot afternoon:

– your older child begs to be allowed to take a new tricycle, and you agree, reluctantly; your younger one is sitting in a push-chair

– you visit the green-grocer and slip two heavy shopping-bags over the handles of the buggy, being careful not to let it tip backwards with the weight

– you then join the queue in the delicatessen and hope for the best

– your child on the tricycle blocks the shop-door, then nearly rides over the foot of a lady coming in; as you apologise to her, you stop concentrating on the child in the buggy, who grabs a jar of beetroot from a ground-level stand and hurls it onto the floor

– you bend down to pick up the bits of glass with one hand, trying to hold the push-chair with the other, but the buggy falls backwards, your younger child screams with indignation, and your apples and oranges roll all over the floor

– one lady remarks to another, 'They don't *discipline* their children these days!'

There is a way of dealing with ridiculous moments like this, which I discovered by accident. I had been thinking about the traditional figure of 'The Fool' (n.b. the picture *Fool and Butterfly* page 49,) who has neither status, power nor reputation. I had also been reading St. Paul's advice in I Corinthians: 'If you think that you are wise in this age, you should become fools so that you may become wise.' (I Corinthians 3: 18 NRSV)

What freedom it must be, I thought to myself, to be like the Fool and to have no public self-image to defend! Not long afterwards, my son's push-chair fell backwards at the shops in a scene not unlike the one described above. And it dawned on me that this was an opportunity to let go of some of the baggage of self-importance and to taste the freedom of the Fool, by laughing with God and saying Yes to the absurd situation in which I found myself.

As parents we often risk making fools of ourselves for the sake of the children. The issue of whether or not to call the doctor is one example. If you phone for help in the middle of the night, your child's pain or discomfort may have disappeared by the time the doctor arrives. (I have always found GP's totally understanding when this has happened to me, but you feel foolish all the same.) If, on the other hand, you *don't* call the doctor, you may be ticked off later for not seeking help. Either way, you have to stick your neck out, make the best decision you can and take the consequences.

Freedom comes when we accept the fact that we are not 'Super-Mum' and 'Super-Dad', gliding calmly round our immaculate and efficient households and never making mistakes. We are vulnerable and harassed, frequently tired and sometimes impatient, and we depend on others more than we would like to admit. Accepting the role of a 'fool for Christ' (I Cor. 4: 10) can be a relief and also give our lives a flavour of fun. Laughing at ourselves always makes us a bit more human.

The Vulnerable Fool
Jesus himself chose a path which was folly in the eyes of the world. Even though he could have enchanted everyone with quasi-magical signs and called up armies of angels to overcome his enemies, Jesus would have none of that, and walked instead the way of pain and rejection (Matthew 4:5–10; Luke 23:8–9). Yet, as St. Paul says, 'God's foolishness is wiser than human wisdom, and God's weakness is stronger than human strength' (ICor: 1: 25 NRSV). Christ is the best Fool who ever lived, and we are closer to him than we think when we ourselves feel foolish and helpless in the eyes of others.

You might like to ponder two contrasting pictures of Christ. The first is a remarkable drawing of the

crucifixion by Cecil Collins. It is quite startling at first, but its many powerful details repay careful attention. Jesus is portrayed as the crowned King of Fools, and his followers on the left, who are also dressed as fools, dance and play their cymbals in a quaint posture. On the right, Christ's enemies stand stiff, rigid and blind, armed to the teeth with sticks and staves, which they imagine will give them power over this supremely free figure, who is stepping down from the cross even as he hangs there. Mary Magdalene's grief is movingly conveyed in the curved lines of her falling hair and the angle of her head.

The second picture (on page 81) is an icon of *Jesus the Saviour*, painted by the early fifteenth-century Russian, Andrei Rublev, for a church in Zvenigorod. The fact that the surface has been damaged makes the painting all the more poignant. It is as if Christ looks at us sorrowfully through the marks which we, the human race, have inflicted on him. In the traditional manner of icons, his mouth is small, representing his inward quietness, and the thick, sturdy neck and blue garment symbolise his humanity. Like us, Jesus is vulnerable and sometimes seen as a fool by the world. Yet his calm, all-seeing eyes show no bitterness but only compassion, and he has tremendous stature as well as tenderness.

Each of these pictures, in its own way, conveys the truth that Jesus is one with us in our fragile humanity; like us, he has known loneliness and suffering. But having taken all our pain into himself, he remains undefeated; and he will never abandon us.

One reason why pictures can help when we are feeling drained, is that they are given, they are *there*, and all we have to do is remain passive while God touches us through them.

The photograph at the end of this chapter is of a small carving of Julian of Norwich, which features on a meditation card entitled *Healing the Pain*[3]. I suggest that you look at it for a while, before reading the following dialogue, which goes with the picture:

'My child, what is it that troubles you? You look full of pain and anxiety.'

'I am full of dread and near to despair. The journey

has been for me one fall after another. I am bruised and tired, and it seems to me now a waste of time to have started at all.' . . .

'But, dearest child, the Lord does not want you to despair like this. However many falls you have had, whether they be your own fault, or whether they be caused by the blows from life that you have received, his love for you is like a rock. None of your falling can harm or alter it.'

'How can this be so? I am wretched and unholy, full of weakness, unlovely and unlovable.'

'You must forget how you feel about yourself; only look at him and see how he feels about you. He wants to assure you of his love. All the hurt and distress that has come to you only moves him to love you more. If you come to him, he will not blame you for your weakness or your blindness. He wants to surround you with his love. Only come to him, and his tender touch will restore you.'[4]

A SPACE FOR STILLNESS

Before you start . . . see page 30

Ψ Read the section *Love Unlimited* (page 76) up to, 'This is the miracle of the Gospel.' Take time to imagine the initial scene in the Pharisee's house. Listen to the sounds, smell the food, watch the people there as they talk and eat. Then look at the expressions on their faces when the woman comes in. Put yourself in her place. How do you perceive it all? How do you feel? What effect do Jesus' words have on you? Stay with your reactions to the scene, and let Jesus love and heal you through this story.

88

Ψ Read slowly the passage from Deuteronomy quoted on page 80 and allow the words to be spoken directly to you, in the way I suggest.

Ψ Meditate on the passage from Isaiah quoted on page 82. Rest in the knowledge that you are infinitely precious in God's eyes.

Ψ Read the first part of the section *The Vulnerable Fool* on pages 84 to 86 about the picture *The Crucifixion* by Cecil Collins (up to the words 'the angle of her head'). Look at that picture (on page 85). See the pain of Christ, e.g. in the stretched-out arms and cruel thorns. Feel the grief of Mary Magdalene.

Ponder the rigid blindness of the authorities on the one side, and the dancing of the 'fools for Christ' on the other.

Think about the infinite strength of Jesus in his moment of utter weakness, and ask God to be with you when you feel weak and vulnerable.

Ψ Read the second part of the section *The Vulnerable Fool* on page 86, 87 up to 'he will never abandon us.' and pray with Rublev's icon *Jesus the Saviour* (on page 81). Ask God to help you to use the icon as a doorway into the presence of Christ; let him look at you with his eyes of love.

Ψ Use the carving of Julian of Norwich (pictured opposite in the way I suggest on pages 86 and 87.

It's a miracle if you do arrive on time.

CHAPTER 6

Going To Church With Our Children

When the chief priests and the teachers of the law saw the wonderful things Jesus did, and the children shouting in the temple area, 'Hosanna to the Son of David!' they were indignant. 'Do you hear what these children are saying?' they asked him. 'Yes,' replied Jesus, 'have you never read, 'From the lips of children and infants you have ordained praise'?' (Matt. 21: 15–16 NIV)

One of the biggest challenges to Christian parents is the adventure of taking our children with us to church. Our experiences vary considerably, because the churches themselves differ so much. Some congregations provide a carpet and soft toys, where children plus Dad and Mum can participate in a relaxed way in a lively and often noisy service. At the other end of the scale, you can bring your young family into a church and feel that every bump, whisper and wriggle is an intrusion into the worship. Most churches fall somewhere between these two extremes. And no matter how welcoming the congregation may be, most of us feel some anxiety when our children squeal or cry, making us wonder whether we should take them out for a while.

If we do carry our squawking offspring into the churchyard, we will probably feel frustrated at having to miss part of the service, especially when our spiritual diet is already meagre. We may also feel resentful because somebody turned round and glared when we were desperately trying to interest our child in a quiet activity. One mother tells me that she even received black looks when her children were colouring (with the sheets of paper on the wooden pews). The sound of crayons echoed round the stone building like the panting of a dog!

If we have moved heaven and earth to get to a service and end up in the churchyard, we can easily feel discouraged about coming *en famille* to public worship at all. And we may feel a tinge of envy at other parents, whose children never seem to move or make a sound, while ours are apparently incapable of staying either still or quiet. It's even worse if our own children were not keen to come in the first place.

What, then, do we do with our shattered nerves and negative emotions at this Sunday worship, which is supposed to be an uplifting start to the week?

Offer the effort of getting there
Until you've experienced it, you have no idea what a super-human effort it can be to bring your family to church at all, let alone on time! The baby's feeds have to be fitted around, and sometimes into, the service-times. And just as you're all on the door-step ready to go, you can guarantee that you will

smell the tell-tale whiff of a dirty nappy, or that somebody's only decent pair of trainers will be thickly clogged with mud . . . so you arrive late yet again.

If your husband or wife happens to be clergy, your job is even harder. Your spouse will have gone on ahead to church, so that you have to cope single-handed with getting everyone clean and dressed, finding the bag of 'silent' toys, making sure the older children have their musical instruments, sorting out last-minute arguments and locking up. It's a miracle if you *do* arrive on time, and even more amazing if you are calm and composed when you finally sink into your seat.

I have found that the only way to survive family church-going is to make the sheer effort of getting there into an offering to God. This helps me to move away from the notion that my participation in the service is somehow less valuable because I have arrived in such a harassed state. The frantic rush involved in coming to church can itself be a gift, placed on the altar like the bread and wine of the Eucharist. Because bread is such an ordinary commodity, it has become for me a link between my own mundane preoccupations and the offering of the bread of Communion.

I have often felt a hypocrite, coming to worship God straight after being so irritable with the children. But I now realise that it is right to be there and to offer myself *as I am*, fraught nerves and all, so that Christ can love, forgive and transform me. God wants us to come to him as we are, and not in some falsely pious attitude. He knows that we genuinely want to worship, and to bring our family into that experience.

Excluded?

But what about those bleak moments when we end up walking round outside with our child (or sheltering in the porch if it's raining) and feeling cut off from the fellowship inside? One way to deal with this is to make that time into a prayer for others, for example:

'Lord, I offer this frustration for all people who are pushed around, criticised, or marginalised; for all who can't sleep, have no home, or are at the end of their tether.'

Another fruitful use of this time is to make it into an offering for the preacher, if you've come out during the sermon. On one occasion I had to preach over the top of a child who squealed right the way through my talk, and I know how difficult that is. Under these circumstances taking your child out is a real help to the preacher, as well as to those in the congregation who have hearing-aids and can hear nothing if there is background noise. But there are other ways of dealing with this situation, such as having a warm and comfortable room available on or near church premises. No parents should be obliged to feel constantly banished to a chilly church-exterior.

When it is hard to concentrate

Another difficulty for fathers and mothers is that we are constantly distracted from the content of the service because of the need to keep our children occupied. This again can make us feel guilty for not giving the attention to God that we feel we should. We are back in our mental prison, pad-locked by our view of 'the only correct way' to pray in church.

People who come to church without young children are able to give their undivided attention to what is going on. But we are not; there is no blame in this, it is a simple fact. And God knows that. He doesn't judge us for it, even if we are criticised by some of the congregation or are busy blaming ourselves. As long as we offer to God our honest intention to be *there*, sharing in the worship of the whole body of Christ, that is what matters.

Worship is not just something *we* do. God is active too, and he will do his work in us when we come to worship, perhaps in ways we don't realise at the time, even when the children are scrambling all over us. God surely doesn't keep a record-book, monitoring the number of sentences to which we have listened during a service. It is the love and commitment with which we come to church that counts, children or no children.

Just as sick people rely on the prayers of others when they are too ill to pray themselves, so we depend on our fellow Christians when we have small children with us, letting the congregation carry and support us through the prayers and flow of the worship. This may be a blow to our pride, but it's good to accept our limitations and our need of each other.

The fact that we cannot cope on our own is another reason why the Eucharist is particularly helpful. The sacrament does not depend on us alone. It is something that Jesus is doing. As the minister or priest re-enacts the events of the Last Supper, Jesus offers us new life and healing. He gives this freely, however preoccupied or unworthy we may be. Our part is to come and receive him, letting him work in us as he wants.

Laughing with God

God must delight in the hilarious situations that our children create in church. I wonder how many young worshippers have pointed out, 'There's Jesus!' at the sight of a bearded bishop, or have uttered a fervent 'Amen' two seconds after everybody else. Countless clergy children must have broken free of the watchful eye of their other parent and whizzed happily up to the front shouting, 'Daddy, Daddy!' or 'Mummy, Mummy!'

One Easter morning, my husband, who is a vicar, sang some extra words of praise in the liturgy. During the few seconds of silence that followed, my five-year old asked in shrill tones, 'Why is Daddy shouting?'

And what *do* you do when a favourite soft ball rolls just out of reach, under the legs of a respectable lady who is sitting, eyes tightly shut, rapt in prayer?

I suspect that in heaven there is much palm-waving mirth and liturgical fun, inspired by the children and shared with us all. We can glimpse it now if we have eyes to see. And if we miss the joke, God is still laughing.

Angels fly and children laugh because they take themselves lightly. Adults have to learn.[1]

*There is, you could say, a babybasher
in us all!*

CHAPTER 7

We Are All Connected

Beloved, let us love one another; for love is from God; everyone who loves is born of God and knows God . . . God is love, and those who abide in love abide in God, and God abides in them. (I John 4:7, 16b. NRSV)

As human beings our lives are interwoven, and each of our actions, however small, affects the world as a whole. Whenever we behave kindly and unselfishly, we contribute to the healing and well-being of all people. Conversely, our blindness and sin add to the world's distress and dis-ease. No event happens in total isolation, least of all when we are with our children. Therefore, when we care for our own family, there is a sense in which we are doing it for all the children on earth.

This fact of our human one-ness opens up several ways of praying, not only for our own families, but also on a wider scale. The practical tasks which we do as a normal part of looking after our own children can be a place where we pray for children such as the urchins driven by desperation to live in the sewers of Brazil, or the young lad, Rashid, pictured on page 100 who was wounded after picking up a mine in Afghanistan. 'The whole of mankind is wonderfully helped by what you are doing, in ways you do not understand,' writes an anonymous author of the fourteenth century[1]. He is talking about quiet prayer, but his words are equally applicable to our attempts to pray for others out of the middle of our everyday life.

When we are unkind or thoughtless with our own

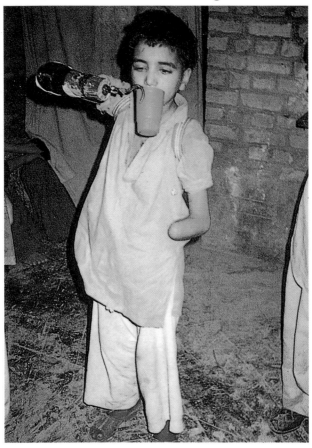

family, we are a part, however small, of the world-wide misusing of children by adults. We are all involved, whether we like it or not, and our prayers for forgiveness can have a corporate as well as a personal meaning. I have sometimes heard people saying things like, 'I can understand baby-bashing now! My child doesn't know what nights are for!' There is, you could say, a baby-basher in us all. It's not that we make a habit of carrying round a sledge-hammer with which to attack our unfortunate brood! But there are times when we are so tired and strained that a frightening surge of anger, along with the desire to hit out, wells up inside us. We all have in us the potential for loss of control, and even violence, and we need to recognise this when we pray for people who have reached their wits' end and damaged their children badly. It is part of our job as Christians to feel the pain of all this and to bring it to God, asking for his mercy and healing on behalf of us all. We are all wounded and broken, and there is darkness inside every one of us; that is what makes us brothers and sisters.[2]

We belong to each other
There is another link between us. We share a common source of life, and depend on the single creative energy which comes from God, just as trees in a field draw on the same supply of water from beneath the surface. What affects one person affects us all. This bond between human beings world-wide can again add depth to our intercession.

For many years now I have prayed for four brave women from Indonesia; Sulami, Sudjinah, Sri Ambar Rukmiati and Suharti Harsono, who were imprisoned for between fifteen and seventeen years in the

1960's and 1970's, simply for helping the children of political prisoners. Even though they are out of gaol, they still cannot be employed in government services or 'vital industries'; they also have to report regularly to the military authorities, and are not allowed to travel freely.

Praying for them over the years has had a curious effect on me. I have felt increasingly close to them, and have sensed that God has blessed *me* through them. Intercession has become a two-way channel of love, and I believe that their suffering has been for the sake of my children as well as for those families in Indonesia. These women are the strong ones, and not I; praying for them has become a privilege and a source of inspiration.

In spite of the continuing restrictions to their freedom, there is a power of love at work in their lives which goes beyond space and time, and which, I believe, comes from God. The spirit of courage and compassion for innocent children shown by Sulami and her friends is still free and at large in the world. No amount of official bullying or petty padlocks can stop the care they have generated or the prayers in which they are now taken up. They are part of my life; my children belong to them, just as, through prayer, the children of Indonesian prisoners belong to me.

All this helps me when my attempts at intercession feel futile and I feel helpless to *do* anything for people in trouble. God uses the fact that we are bonded as human beings to make us channels of blessing for each other when we pray. This mystery lies behind St. Paul's observation, 'If we suffer, it is for your help and salvation; if we are helped, then you too are helped, and given the same strength to endure with patience the same sufferings that we also endure . . . just as you share in our sufferings, you also share in the help we receive' (II Cor. 1:6, 7b). Sometimes the only thing we have in common with those for whom we pray is our human weakness and helplessness – but that is itself a bond. An Anglican nun, Mother Mary Clare, whose life was steeped in prayer, has helped me to understand this mystery more deeply. She writes, 'When Christians, as men and women of this torn and anguished world, come to stand before God who is our life, all creation begins, through us, to receive again the gift of life.'[3]

When we feel inadequate and ground down by the demands of parenthood in our own lives, we are sharing, to some degree, the experience of millions of parents who struggle to bring up their children against all kinds of odds. So we can offer our own difficulties in an act of intercession for parents world-wide, from those whose are so poor that they can hardly feed their children, to those whose teen-agers are facing the pressures of commercialism, drink, drugs and sex. No prayer like this is wasted. We don't know how it works, but we are asked to trust that God uses these prayers to bless others. 'Have no anxiety about anything,' writes St. Paul again, this time from prison, 'but in everything by prayer and supplication, with thanksgiving, let your requests be made known to God' (Phil. 4:6).

Lord, I offer my daily life with my children,
as a prayer
for all the children of the world,
especially those who are
unloved,
maltreated,
sexually abused,
starving,
lonely,
bullied,
orphaned,
or afraid.

Lord, I offer my struggle with the demands of
parenthood
as a prayer
for other parents,
those who face similar difficulties,
and those whose problems are different.

Lord, I offer my delight in my children
as a prayer
for childless couples
bereaved parents,
single parents who ache for someone to share
the load,
adopted children who have been told the truth
too late,
women who have had abortions,
aborted babies,
and for all the secure and contented children
too.

'The whole of nature touches and intertwines ...
We all share in this universe through one and the
same rhythm, universal gravity ... We are all in
contact and we are all incomplete; everything in
nature is incomplete, and offers itself to another
... The whole of creation groans with us, as Paul
said, and we cannot rest till we find God; towards
him all creatures strain, and only in him can the
universe find rest.' (Ernesto Cardenal)[4]

Spirit of Christ, sanctify me!
Accept and transform
my small energy of desire
that it may become
part of your great energy of desire
for the redemption of the world.
(Evelyn Underhill)[5]

A SPACE FOR STILLNESS

Before you start . . . see page 30

Ψ Read the first section of Chapter 7 on pages 99 to 101. Make a list of the thoughts that come straight to mind under the headings 'Good things that happen with my children' and 'Bad things that happen with my children.' Then offer each of these as prayer for other members of the human family, in whatever way God leads you.

Ψ Use slowly and thoughtfully the prayer on page 104.

Ψ Ponder the words of Ernesto Cardenal, and use Evelyn Underhill's prayer (page 105), or use your own words if you prefer, in an act of commitment of your life to God.

We feel bewildered and alone.

CHAPTER 8

Cuddling And Letting Go

'As one whom his mother comforts, so I will comfort you,' says the Lord. (Isaiah 66:13)

Cuddling our children is one of the greatest delights of parenthood, and is also vitally important. It is said that new-born babies who are never picked up or given the warmth of human contact can become ill or even die, in spite of being adequately nourished. And it would be unbearable if we, for our part, were denied the chance to hold our children close to us, whatever their age.

From this we can glimpse something of the way in which God loves us. He cares for us and enfolds us in his love, whether we are hurt or thrilled, exhilarated or tired, pleased with something we've done or miserable after making a hash of things. So when we pray, we have a chance to rest in God's arms, like a peaceful child on its mother's lap (Psalm 131:2).

I spent some time recently with a friend and her ten-week-old baby. As she gently rubbed his back, holding him against her shoulder and rocking him, the special joy of cuddling small babies came back to me, and it reminded me of the tender bond between ourselves and God. It is sad that the marvellous insights about the motherhood in God's nature can send such alarm-bells ringing through the churches. We don't have to deny God's fatherhood, or devalue the ministry of men, in order to draw on the riches of this thoroughly Scriptural truth:

'Can a woman forget her suckling child?' says God in Isaiah 49:15. 'Even these may forget, yet I will not forget you.'

Jesus himself wept over Jerusalem not long before he died, and said,

'How often would I have gathered your children together, as a hen gathers her brood under her wings, and you would not!' (Luke 13:34, 19:41)

As early as the fourteenth century, Julian of Norwich took up this theme of Christ as our mother in a startlingly vivid passage:

'Our true Mother Jesus gives us birth to joy and endless life.

He carries us within himself in love, and labours until full term, so that he could suffer the sharpest throes . . .

The mother can give her child suck from her milk, but our precious Mother Jesus can feed us with himself; and he does it most graciously and most tenderly with the Blessed Sacrament which is the precious food of true life.

The mother can lay the child tenderly on her breast, but our tender Mother Jesus can more intimately lead us into His blessed Breast by His sweet open side.[1]

Letting go

There is, however, another side to loving. As well as holding our children and keeping them safe, we have to let them go, sometimes at considerable cost to ourselves. We all struggle to find the delicate balance between protecting them on the one hand, and giving them the space and freedom to find their feet on the other. This process of necessary separation begins as soon as the umbilical cord is cut, but it becomes more apparent when a child is weaned, learns to walk, travels on a bus or train for the first time, and goes to late parties as a teenager. Indeed all loving, and not only that between parents and children, involves allowing the other to be free, and resisting the temptation to possess them in any way.

There is a similar pattern in our relationship with God. Sometimes we sense that he is very close, but, at other times, he seems to withdraw so that we feel bewildered and alone. Looking at our children's experience may help us to understand what is happening to us. It can be alarming for a small child not to have its mother's hand to cling to. At the mothers'-and-toddlers' group, for example, the mums stay at the side, and if the little ones want a turn on the exciting-looking climbing-frame in the middle of the room they have to venture out on their own. Yet Mummy is always there, even when they lose sight of her for a few frightening moments and dissolve into panic-stricken tears.

This throws some light on the way our perception of God's presence can vary so much, and helps us to understand why we sometimes feel bereft, like the tearful child at the playgroup, and cry out with the psalmist, 'How long O Lord? Will you hide yourself for ever?' (Ps. 89: 46 NRSV)

God never does stop loving us. But he doesn't clutch or force us into a celestial 'smother-love' either. Instead he holds us with a lightness of touch that is almost imperceptible, and which springs from his infinite gentleness. And at times he allows us to step out into a strange and unknown territory where we have to trust him more deeply.

Two psalms can encourage us here. The first is Psalm 131, which contains the marvellous verse:

'I have calmed and quieted my soul
like a weaned child with its mother.' (v. 2 NRSV)

The word 'weaned', which is unfortunately lost in some translations, is important. The child portrayed here is no longer a suckling infant, as we might have expected, but is learning to live without the special intimacy of breast-feeding. The break has been made, yet he is still secure and at peace in the knowledge of his mother's care for him. There is a perfect balance here between cuddling and letting go, which reflects something of the mystery of what happens between ourselves and God.

The other is Psalm 139, which reassures us that God is still there, watching and loving us, even when we wander off, like a lost toddler, to the farthest edges of existence.

'If I ascend into heaven you are there:
If I make my bed in the grave, you are there also.
If I spread out my wings towards the morning:
or dwell in the uttermost parts of the sea,
even there your hand shall lead me:
and your right hand shall hold me.' (vv. 7–9)[2]

The Compassionate Father

There may be all sorts of reasons why we *feel* that God is far away. Perhaps we have strayed into an attitude or way of behaving which is not in tune with his will for us, so that he is patiently waiting for us to return to him. Or maybe he is helping us to be more mature in our faith, and less dependent on the good feelings in prayer which are traditionally called 'consolations'. Whatever the cause, we can be certain that he never ceases to care, nor is he far away.

A passage from Hosea conveys powerfully this paradoxical nature of our relationship with God:

'When Israel was a child, I loved him . . .
I was the one who taught Israel to walk,
I took my people up in my arms . . .
I drew them to me with affection and love.
I picked them up and held them to my cheek;
I bent down and fed them.' (From Hosea 11: 1, 3–4 GNB)

This picture is full of contrasts. When the loving father teaches his child to walk, he has to let him go, so that the child can take his own precarious steps and risk falling over – even if he is on the end of a harness, as some translations suggest. But the father will keep a watchful eye on him all the same. Then we see the father taking the infant up in his arms and drawing him affectionately to his cheek. This is a marvellous portrayal of how God both allows us to be free and holds us in his care.

There is also a mixture of joy and pain in God himself: joy in his delight in the beloved child, but anguish when the child Israel does not respond to his love:

'I took my people up in my arms,
but they did not acknowledge that I took care
of them.' (Hosea 11:3)

Later verses in the chapter continue this theme:

'How can I give you up, Israel?
How can I abandon you? . . .
My heart will not let me do it.
My love for you is too strong.' (Hosea 11:8)

As human parents we make many mistakes with our
children, but we can trust God absolutely in the way
he handles us. When it seems that he is distant and
remote, passages like the one above from Hosea help
us to remember how dearly we are loved. Nothing at
all, as St. Paul reminds us, can separate us from the
love of God in Christ[3]: nothing, in heaven or on earth,
in nurseries or kitchen sinks, in homework crises or
in a house full of our children's noisy friends, in
sleepless nights or jam-packed days – *nothing*!

God our Mother,
Living Water,
River of Mercy,
Source of Life,
in whom we live
and move
and have our being,
who quenches our thirst,
refreshes our weariness,
bathes
and washes

and cleanses
our wounds,
be for us always
a fountain of life,
and for all the world
a river of hope
springing up in the midst
of the deserts of despair.
(Miriam Therese Winter)[4]

'Father, I let go into you,
for underneath are your everlasting arms.'
(Richard Harries, based on Deut. 33:27)[5]

A SPACE FOR STILLNESS

Before you start . . . see page 30

Ψ Read the first section in Chapter 8 (pages 109 to 110). Listen again to the words from Scripture quoted in that section, and open up to receive God's love for you.

Ψ Read the section *Letting Go* (pages 111 to 113). Use the verse from Psalm 131, 'I have calmed and quieted my soul, like a weaned child with its mother,' as a thread-word to lead you into silence.

Ψ Read the section *The Compassionate Father* on pages 114 to 115. Turn your face towards God, who is waiting to draw you to himself. Ask him to deepen your trust in him. Stay with his promise that *nothing at all* can separate you from his love.

Ψ Pray the prayers on pages 115 and 116, and let yourself go into God's 'everlasting arms.'

NOTES

INTRODUCTION

1 This incident is related in a letter from Father Gilbert Shaw, quoted in the article 'A Wealthy Place' by Sr Barbara June SLG, in *Fairacres Chronicle* (Summer 1986, Vol. 19, No. 2)

2 Some of the themes in this book also appear in my earlier books, *Heaven in Ordinary* and *Prayer in the Shadows*. But I develop them more fully here, with specific reference to young families, as well as including much new material.

CHAPTER 1 – Rescued From Guilt

1 From Kay Gibbons, quoted with permission

2 Julian of Norwich *Revelations of the Divine Love*, in a translation by Fr. John-Julian OJN entitled *A Lesson of Love*, D.L.T. 1988, p. 11

3 There is also much helpful material for use during quiet-times in *Open to God* and *The Smile of Love* by Joyce Huggett, Hodder and Stoughton 1989 and 1990

4 Jennifer Rees Larcombe *Leaning on a Spider's Web*, Hodder & Stoughton 1991 Pages 155–6

CHAPTER 2 – Life's Relentlessness

[1] *Fairacres Chronicle*, Winter 1989, Vol. 22 No.3, in the article 'Time: Prison or Path to Freedom' page 12

[2] *Conversations and Letters of Brother Lawrence*, Mowbray, 1980, p. 23

[3] See my book *Prayer in the Shadows*, Collins Fount 1990 pp. 15–16

[4] *A Prisoner and Yet* by Corrie tern Boom, pp. 29–30, CLC. My italics.

[5] From the original prayer by General Lord Jacob Astley (1579–1652) before the battle of Edgehill. In *The Oxford Book of Prayer* Ed. George Appleton, OUP 1985 No. 317

[6] Quoted in *Holiness* by Donald Nicholl p. 106. DLT 1981

CHAPTER 3 – Attentiveness

[1] I owe this insight to William Barry S.J. in his book *You and God*, Paulist Press 1987 p. 20

[2] See *Perfect Fools* by John Saward, OUP 1980, p.ix

[3] *Aurora Leigh* Bk. vii. Quoted in the *Oxford Dictionary of Quotations* OUP 1948

[4] Harper & Row 1988 p.xiii and p. 78

[5] Prayer cards (in colour) available from the Community of St. Clare, St. Mary's Convent, Freeland, Witney, Oxford OX8 8AJ

[6] Fr. John-Julian, op cit, Chapter 6, pp. 15–16

[7] From *Tools for Meditation* p. 28 Grail Publications

CHAPTER 4 – Thread-words

1 See *Heaven in Ordinary*, Chapter 6, McCrimmon 1985

2 Using the old translation in the Authorised Version

3 From an address in an Advent Service on BBC I T.V. from Norwich Cathedral, December 1991

4 *Beguine Spirituality* Ed. Fiona Bowie p. 55. SPCK 1989

5 From a Christmas card produced by SLG Press, Convent of the Incarnation, Fairacres, Oxford, OX4 1TB. The quote is adapted from a sentence in *Sceptrum Regale: Life towards the Transcendent* by Mother Maria, page 23: 'The place of rest is the being-loved of God.'

6 Exact source unknown

7 Quoted in *The Oxford Book of Prayer* No. 276 Ed. George Appleton OUP 1988

8 Some translations, such as the Good News Bible, have lost the pattern and impact of these two pairs of words. The RSV is more accurate.

9 Maria Boulding, *Marked for Life* SPCK Triangle 1979. p. 84.

10 Adapted from a prayer in *Journey Within* by F.C. Happold DLT 1968 page 98

CHAPTER 5 – When We Feel Inadequate

1 I first wrote about this in an article 'Two-Way Arrows, Prayer in a Busy Life' in *Home and Family*, published by the Mothers' Union, Sept. – Nov. 1989.

2 Fr. John-Julian, op cit, Chap. 49 p. 112

3 Fr. John-Julian, op cit, Artist Connie Cook. Picture

reproduced with permission from the collection of Lord St. John of Fawsley. Words reproduced with permission from Mirfield Publications Ltd.

[4] This is No. 13 in a series of Picture Meditations, all of which are helpful, and are available from Mirfield Publications Ltd., House of the Resurrection, Mirfield, W. Yorkshire WF14 OBN.

CHAPTER 6 – Going To Church With Our Children

[1] Adapted from a sentence in Macrina Wiedekehr's book *A Tree Full of Angels*, Harper & Row 1988 p. 134: 'Angels fly because they take themselves lightly.'

CHAPTER 7 – We Are All Connected

[1] *The Cloud of Unknowing*, Ed. Clifton Wolters, Penguin 1961. p.53

[2] I have learned much about this from the wisdom of Jean Vanier, based on his experience in communities with the mentally handicapped; see, for example, *The Broken Body*, DLT 1988 Part 3

[3] *Encountering the Depths*, DLT 1981 p. 80

[4] *Love*, Search Press, London 1974 p. 19–21

[5] Exact source unknown

CHAPTER 8 – Cuddling And Letting Go.

[1] Fr. John-Julian, op cit, Chapter 60 page 157

[2] ASB 1989 SPCK

[3] cf. Romans 8: 38–39

[4] *A Lent Sourcebook II* p.65 LTP 1990

[5] *Praying Round the Clock*, Mowbray 1983 p. 134

Every effort has been made to obtain permission for use of copyright material. I apologise if correction is needed, and will amend any reprint of this book should this be neccessary.

PHOTOGRAPH PERMISSIONS

All cartoons, both on the front cover and throughout the book, are by Paul Judson, Lobely Hill, Gateshead, and are used with permission.

The photographs, all used with permission are:

p8 Angela Ashwin.

p17 From the film *Jesus of Nazareth*, directed by Franco Zeffirelli, c ITC Entertainment, London.

p25 Yorkshire Dales, c BBC Radio Vision *Quest: Behold I Make All Things New;* slide no. 31.

p37 *Wheatfield with Lark* by Vincent van Gogh (1853–1890), Vincent van Gogh Foundation, Van Gogh Museum, Amsterdam.

p49 *Fool and Butterfly (1985)* by Cecil Collins (1908 – 1989), c Mrs Elisabeth Collins.

p81 *The Saviour from the Deessis of Zvenigorod* by Andrei Rublev (c. 1370 – 1430), Tretyakov gallery, Mosow. Reproduced with permission from *Behold the Beauty of the Lord* by Henri Nouwen, Ave Maria Press.

p85 *The Crucifixion* by Cecil Collins (1908 – 1989), c Mrs Elisabeth Collins.

p88 Statuette of Julian of Norwich by Connie Cook, reproduced by permission of The Rt. Hon. Lord St. John of Fawsley.

p96 *The Umbrellas* by Renoir, c The National Gallery, London.

p100 'Rashid' from Afghanistan, The British Red Cross.

p112 Angela Ashwin.

Jim Borst

COMING TO GOD

in the Stillness

'No words can describe, no book explain, what it means to love Jesus' writes Jim Borst. 'We can only know from personal experience. When he visits our heart, it is bathed in the light of truth . . . Those who have tasted Jesus hunger for more. Those who have drunk of him are thirsty for more. But only those who love him are able to fulfil their desires – to know joy in his embrace now and glory later in his kingdom.'

Coming to God, first published in booklet form under the title *A Method of Contemplative Prayer*, has already shown countless readers how to draw closer to God; how to drink in his love. They have discovered that it is a book to be pondered and savoured, practised and prayed.

This revised, illustrated edition provides a stage by stage introduction to a variety of ways of using times of stillness.

'I have read countless books on prayer but I come back time and again to Jim Borst's distilled wisdom. COMING TO GOD is a book I would like to place into the hands of all who are serious about deepening their prayer life.'
JOYCE HUGGETT

'My sisters and I want to thank you for giving us Jesus, the Bread of Life and his Good News through your words.'
MOTHER TERESA